OLD IS IN

D0860634

OLD IS IN

A Guide for Aging Boomers

by Eric Nicol

THE DUNDURN GROUP
TORONTO

Editorial Director: Anthony Hawke
Copy-Editor: Jennifer Bergeron
Design: Andrew Roberts
Printer: Webcom

Library and Archives Canada Cataloguing in Publication

Nicol, Eric, 1919-
   Old is in : a guide for aging boomers / Eric Nicol.

ISBN 1-55002-524-4

   1. Aging--Humor. 2. Baby boom generation--Humor. 3. Older people--Humor. I. Title.

PS8527.I35O44 2004   C818'.5402   C2004-903138-4

1   2   3   4   5   08   07   06   05   04

 Conseil des Arts du Canada Canada Council for the Arts Canadᾱ

We acknowledge the support of the Canada Council for the Arts and the Ontario Arts Council for our publishing program. We also acknowledge the financial support of the Government of Canada through the Book Publishing Industry Development Program and The Association for the Export of Canadian Books, and the Government of Ontario through the Ontario Book Publishers Tax Credit program, and the Ontario Media Development Corporation's Ontario Book Initiative.

Printed and bound in Canada.
Printed on recycled paper.

www.dundurn.com

Dundurn Press
8 Market Street Suite 200
Toronto, Ontario, Canada
M5E 1M6

Gazelle Book Services Limited
White Cross Mills
Hightown, Lancaster, England
LA1 4X5

Dundurn Press
2250 Military Road
Tonawanda NY
U.S.A. 14150

OLD IS IN

Table of Contents

The White Wave of Boomers

It is the biggest social question of our time: Will the baby boom generation be able to handle old age as well as its parents did? Namely, those of us who lived through the Great Depression and graduated from the School of Hard Knocks. Summa cum lumps.

People now over seventy took a required course in self-reliance because there was no vibrator on the market except the Model T Ford. Our only support group was the family, which was the reason so many of us volunteered for the Second World War.

In contrast, the baby boomer is accustomed to having all of his or her problems taken care of by the Government. Big Momma. She of the broad mind and big teats. This is the generation that sought eternal values in the stock market and immortality at the fitness centre.

Now, the sex drive has shifted into neutral. Parts of the body that once enjoyed vigorous athletic activities — downhill skiing, league football, necking in the back seat of a Jeep — suddenly complain at routine exercises such as raising a question.

Hail, Geezer! Remember in high school, how you couldn't wait to become a senior? Well, it appears you'll finally make it. You'll have to turn sixty-five to do it, but through an exemplary combination of cunning and good luck, you will graduate into senescence.

Now what? How do you cope with continued existence when there is little chance of a TV career as an exhibit on *Antiques Roadshow*?

Well, you may take comfort in having lots of company in this class of the no-credits course. Being old is *in*. Getting out is less popular, but no stage of life is perfect.

This is why it is a good idea to be able to recognize that the declining years mean more than saying "no" to everything.

"You're only as old as you feel." A rubber index. Forget it.

"Oldness is highly relative." True (i.e., the more relatives you have, the faster you age).

So what *are* the clear indications that the Grim Reaper is trying you on for scythe?

First of all, clinical trials show that oldness is the result of aging. If we didn't age, all of us would be Peter Pans and getting arrested for flying into little girls' bedrooms. This is why it is a good idea to recognize the signs of aging before we become daft, which is the condition of being senile without a sizable estate.

For starters, chronological age means nothing. Especially if you lie about it. (Some parts of your body may even believe you, after a few drinks.) Or you may just "ish" the number ("I'm sixtyish, seventyish, deadish…").

In the same varicose vein: the traditional marker for longevity has been that a man should die at par for the course: about seventy-two, give or take a couple of strokes. A woman scores a few more years because she doesn't drive as hard.

Much to the delight of life insurance companies, the lifespan's off-ramp has been extended. It is no longer unusual for a person to live to be a hundred. To get the attention of the media, you need to be at least a passable Scrabble score — over 110. Centenarians are as common as houseflies, which they also attract. As for living into your nineties — Yawnsville. No one marvels. So you got lucky driving the freeway, so what?

Also, even though we ourselves have turned sixty-five (at least once), there are days when we feel young enough to make fools of ourselves. And be excused as a juvenile, making a late bloomer.

Much clearer are:

Posted Signs of Aging

1. Becoming sexually aroused is a major project. Possibly requiring a hard hat.
2. Your doctor ruptures himself lifting your file.
3. As a driver, the only time you exceed the speed limit is when passing a cemetery.
4. If you're a guy you avoid bus travel because elderly ladies offer you their seat.
5. Nobody tries to sell you a long-term bond.
6. Or buy you a drink.
7. You avoid visiting museums, in case someone mistakes you for an exhibit.
8. You know that pain is better than having no sensation at all.
9. An eye doctor tells you that the reason you are having problems with your eyes is that you have gone blind.
10. An arthritic view of shoelaces causes you to wear slippers on all occasions except family weddings.
11. You wear black, all-season socks, and once installed you never take them off, because reaching them is arduous.

12. You go to bed with the birds, you get up with the birds, and the time in between is for the birds.

13. Faced with the staircase to Heaven, you figure it's easier to go to Hell.

14. When you get sick, the only get-well card you receive is from your life insurance company.

15. You are subject to so many body aches, they have to take a number.

16. From experience you know that all friendly strangers are realtors.

17. Your Memory Lane has degraded to a back alley, while the Street of Dreams is potholed with nightmares.

18. You see Hell as just an extension of the microwave oven.

19. You do not ask for whom the siren wails. You may not want to know.

20. The sight of you causes complete strangers to cross themselves.

The Alternatives

The surest way to avoid becoming old is, of course, to die young. (A person can also die when middle-aged, but it is harder to tell.)

"Whom the gods love die young." Plautus is credited with saying it first, indicating that the ancient Romans too had bladder problems.

The bleak wheeze was repeated by Wordsworth, Byron (he had a bum leg), and other poets who were having a bad hair day. Significantly, all of these glum observers were guys. This means that:

a) women refuse to admit to being old,

b) the gods don't try to mess with the gentle sex, or

c) male poets don't have much to write about.

So, every senior should consider the following scenario: One night, he wakes up feeling uncomfortably warm and finds Mephistopheles sitting on his chest.

"Greetings, sucker!" says the Devil, who also has bad breath. "Have I got a deal for *you*! I grant you eternal youth as a scratch golfer, with the ability to play hot trombone, in exchange for your soul when you hop the twig. If you accept this offer without thinking, I'll also throw in a cool set of abs."

How does our fusty Faust respond to this temptation, if allergic to sulphanilamide? The offer looks foolproof. Signing over your soul to Satan seems academic if you are enjoying eternal youth and a personal parking space. A person could still have a fatal accident, of course, and have his soul go straight to Hell, but it cuts down on the paperwork.

Another option: Inspired by Oscar Wilde's celebrated novel, the death-dodger has his portrait painted by someone who is not recommended by the Better Business Bureau. The idea is to hide the portrait in a closet where the image grows old and revolting while the subject remains ever youthful despite indulgence in a wide variety of vices and perversions that ordinarily would be very bad for the complexion.

Like most other deals offered by portrait studios, the one that Dorian Gray bought into just proved that an aging person should either avoid depraved conduct or be very careful about what he puts in the closet.

So the vital question is: Would having eternal youth offer any advantage over being stuck in an elevator with a six-hundred-pound gorilla? Especially if one is a permanent *teenager*. (One good thing about being old is that you are not obsessed with losing your virginity. Either you have already lost it or are on the shortlist for election to the papacy.)

Another cure for oldness: today's youth seems bound to indulge in "extreme" sports. Other than dating redheads. The invention of the skateboard and other similar equipment has opened up a whole new world of opportunity for kids to avoid maturity. Those of us who missed it may never know the thrill of skiing in an avalanche area, rafting down rain-swollen rapids, or driving a car in downtown Vancouver. Cruel fate!

Actuarial Discrimination

"My wife had her face lifted."

"Really? Why would anybody want to steal a thing like that?"

No question: women age better than men. Their face develops a better class of wrinkle. Life has given old ladies laugh lines and old men exit lines.

Old men commit suicide more often than old women. Well, actually, they commit suicide only once, but it seems like more.

Why is this? How do women manage to age graciously, while men hang on grimly to the illusion that the expanding bald spot is temporary, caused by a surge of testosterone?

When we say "There's no fool like an old fool," we're talking Tom, Dick, and Harry, not Tess, Deb, and Hilda. Women mature like French wine and cheese, while men age more like meatloaf.

Women enjoy each other's society more as they get older, while men continue to eye one another as rivals in some endeavour that escapes their mind. When you visit a rest home you see the women residents sitting around together, verbally dismembering relatives, while each old guy sits alone outside in his wheelchair, trying to figure out an escape route.

Say "old hermit" and we automatically think of a guy with years of attitude. Old women are too sociable to avoid company unless their hearing aid is on the blink.

If, out in the woods, we see the sign "TRESPASSERS WILL BE SHOT," we know that the property owner is an old man whose only remaining meaningful relationship is with a double-barrelled shotgun.

Thus all the evidence indicates that women accept the aging process, whereas men still see it as an unnatural affliction, probably caused by their earlier contact with females.

Features of the Fossilized

Seniors would all be able to enjoy the attention given to the younger generation were it not for certain physiological indicators that blab our status as a coeval of T. Rex:

1. Liver spots

These are not spots that appear on the liver, though God knows we wish they were. Other people don't notice our liver, but unless we wear gloves indoors as well as outdoors, people can see the mottled mitt. The skin that nobody loves to touch.

There is no cure for liver spots, because medical researchers are too preoccupied with creating dental strips that whiten teeth. Which have become another highly visible indicator of the living fossil.

2. Yellow ivories

It is hard to say which are the more grievous advertise-
ment of aging: the fallow fangs or the preternaturally
white dentures that can scare people not prepared for
the glare. This is why some older folk confine hilarity
to a thin smile.

3. Nasal gorse

For some reason that medical science seems reluctant to explain, the nostrils wait till we turn sixty-
five to produce this grey eminence — which seems
to have no function other than to discourage
wildlife from accessing the body via the schnoz. The
barber will use a Weed Eater to attack this bracken,
thus encouraging it to grow thicker and inviting
asphyxiation. Some seniors prefer to pull their nose
hair out by the roots, proving that they can still produce tears. The bristles, however, are replaced,
overnight, by an even denser array of honker sedge
that can frighten small children.

4. Tower of Pisa posture

This loss of verticality, induced by an arthritic back, is hard to camouflage by pretending to be always searching the ground for a lost object. No one is inclined to be old, but it happens anyway. Which is why the senior's preferred stance is sitting. During which he does not cross his legs because he knows, from experience, that uncrossing them may require help from a paramedic. (An elderly gentleman will still stand up when approached by a lady, but may need twenty-four hours' notice).

5. Rusted voice

With aging, a man's voice goes higher, while a woman's voice goes baritone. Eventually both have the same pitch, but by then it's game over. This voice change is caused by petrification of the vocal cords, folds in the lining of the larynx whose edges vibrate in the airstream produced either by the lungs or by gas (the geriatric burp).

6. Wrinkles

A wrinkle is a dimple that overdid it. Wrinkles appear only on areas of the body where other people will see them. The private parts don't wrinkle, but this is not evident at most church picnics. Around the eyes, the "laugh-lines" have either lost their sense of humour or become hysterical. The back of the hand looks like a high-altitude photo of the physiognomy of northern Afghanistan. Such wrinkles can be removed by cosmetic surgery, at a very private clinic, but the bill will cause worry lines to appear on your bank statement.

7. Fingernails

They're the only parts of the body that are still growing, and faster than ever. Overnight, fingernails can grow to a length associated with those of the old emperors of China, but without the compensating concubines. The toenails have developed the same projection, and have become as brittle as a Coke bottle. Ordinary nail scissors fail to make an impression, tempting the oldster to use a power saw.

Worse, cutting the nail produces *shrapnel*. This is why it is absolutely essential to wear safety goggles.

Industrial strength. Also rubber gloves. While gowned like a brain surgeon. Because there is going to be blood.

The Gender Gap

As they grow older, men tend to go bald, whereas women just change their hairdresser. For women, menopause occurs between forty and fifty. The male menopause happens over a guy's dead body. Old ladies don't think about sex much, and old men don't think about it at all — except during waking hours. Old married men do not consider deafness to be a drawback. Old wives see it as life-threatening. The old lady accepts the loss of libido as natural. The old gent believes that his performance in bed could be as good as ever, if only he didn't get dizzy taking off his shoes. Aging women adapt readily to the computer — e-mail, chatlines, etc. — while older men hesitate to surf the Net without a lifejacket. The retired company executive continues to see the ideal laptop to be a blonde secretary.

For reading material, elderly ladies choose novels and short stories written by other women who have no hope of going to bed with anything else. Old men prefer fiction in the form of autobiography, political memoirs, or other comic books.

Usually outliving their husbands, old wives commonly replace the spouse with a small dog. Widowers choose a cat, because cats don't need to be walked, washed, dewormed, or licensed, and won't bark at them for leaving the seat up.

Politically, old men have lost faith in representative government and find redeeming features in Adolph Hitler. Old ladies see government as a hierarchy of power consisting of:

1. Grandma,
2. daughters-in-law, and
3. any female relative under the age of six.

Retirement — The Beginning of the Ugh

Poured from the blender that is life are the mixed feelings people have about retirement. Nearly everyone looks forward to retiring in the sense of going to bed. Most seniors retire night after night, with nothing but good feelings towards their mattress.

Quite different are the sentiments of the sixty-five-year-old compulsorily retired from his or her job. Such retirement may be one life change that a person cannot afford. Statistics show that 33 percent of

Canadians nearing retirement age are worried that they haven't made adequate financial provisions to maintain their lifestyle, if this includes eating.

People fear that their nest egg is addled. It will produce no chick, or any other form of social life.

Many people approaching sixty suspect that their RRSP — that raspberry in waiting — will prove that the best-laid plans of mice and men work better for the rodents. They realize, too late, that buying lottery tickets was not as smart an investment as buying a house.

So, 18 percent of boomers have gone on record as not planning to retire at all. They hope to drop in the traces, on their expiry date.

Because "a woman's work is never done," retirement doesn't bother women as much as it does men, for whom work can be as important as sex, and usually better paid.

The deskectomy — and physical separation from the office coffee machine — is rarely made less painful by the parting retirement gift of a piece of luggage. The implied message: "Hit the road, Pops!"

Instantly, a company's vigorous sixty-five-year-old worker is transformed into a *pensioner*. The effect on a man is immediate:

- his testes shrink to walnuts,
- he becomes invisible to women, and
- he starts walking like a dork.

Some people are not subject to retirement — like
farmers, who make a point of having no record of
how old they are and go on happily losing money till
they drop in the traces. This, in fact, is the main
advantage of being *self-employed*. If self tries to tell
you that you are too old for the job, you can tell
yourself where you can stuff the retirement and spit
in your own eye. On the other hand, you can be self-
employed and hate your boss. This can lead to psy-
chotic behaviour, such as trying to catch yourself
leaving work early.

Many people try to alleviate retirement by activating:

The Dream Cruise

Nearly everyone, though otherwise sane, dreams of
climaxing a lifetime of toil and struggle — or even
fifty years on welfare — by taking that fabulous cruise

to Alaska. Or the Caribbean. Or the Greek islands, a.k.a The Horrors That Odysseus Missed.

Such is the heavy demand for these pricey suicide missions, by aging persons whose IQ may be above average but whose common sense matches that of a head of lettuce, that shipping lines are putting most of their resources into building bigger and bigger cruise ships, whose launchings create global tsunamis that wipe out entire villages in Bangladesh.

Among the notable features of the super-cruise ship are the ten thousand portholes, none of which open. Thus a passenger may travel for days on the ocean without ever getting a breath of sea air. Every stateroom depends on the ship's air-conditioning system, which draws on the stacks' diesel engine exhaust to reproduce the effect of driving three thousand miles behind a Mack truck. Even the seagulls avoid it.

Cruise ship passengers are discouraged from going on deck to breathe fresh air, because there is no place out there for them to spend whatever life savings they have left after paying the travel fare. Instead of having staterooms large enough for the occupants to fall full-length when overcome by toxic fumes, the cruise liner's interior is devoted to casinos, gift shops, and tiny golf courses where a ball may be rented by the hour.

To cater to the elderly clientele, the most popular, if not the most spacious, accommodation aboard a cruise ship is the hospital. With meals being prepared and served by persons too busy to have washed their hands since leaving the last port of call, the chances are good of a passenger's picking up an exotic bug — Norwalk or some other heir to Black Death.

Yet the passenger will rise, zombie-like, from the sick bay, determined to use the expensive camera hung around his neck to accompany the dead albatross. But his hope of getting a sensational photo of phenomena like an iceberg calving fades when:

- because of fog, the only ice he sees is in a bar bucket;
- the West Indies tour has to be aborted when the captain finds that the Panama Canal is closed for the annual removal of workers dead from Yellow Fever; or
- the passenger's camera is seized by new Turkish island authorities, and his wife is stoned for wearing slacks.

But the real danger for the retiree on his "all-inclusive" tour is running out of traveller's cheques in some country that still has capital punishment. The illusion that one is being loved for oneself, rather than one's cash, is shattered in a matter of seconds. The welcomed visitor instantly becomes a foreigner — something that he may never have experienced in his own land. Educational, yes, but a hazard to the senior who is already on high blood pressure medication.

The pensioner may also be attracted to the "package" tour. It is called a "package" because the traveller ends up looking like something that has been kept too long at a postal station.

Usually the package tour involves travel by bus. The tour bus is an extension of the school bus, but leaves the passenger with the strong feeling of having paid a high price to learn a severe lesson.

The tour bus often has darkened windows, so that people outside can't see the expressions on the faces of the people locked inside.

The bus usually has a driver, who sits in a cubicle insulated against the sounds — moans, cries, hysterical laughter — emitted by the passengers. For tours longer than twenty-four hours, the bus may have a built-in john, for the convenience of passengers who failed to pack, and wear, enough Pampers to soak up Lake Michigan. Using the bus biffy while the bus is bouncing over road repairs is said to be an uplifting experience, though a tad short of visiting the Sistine Chapel.

The experienced bus traveller will prefer to wait till the bus stops at a viewpoint with a wide selection of trees. This is why he avoids the desert tours outside Las Vegas, Nevada.

Choosing a Doctor: A Major Operation

An educational benefit of the dream cruise is that the senior returns home more aware that he or she is too old for that kind of watery safari. Henceforth most of his travel is confined to trips to the doctor. Your doctor should therefore be chosen with more care than other intimate relationships, such as wife or husband.

Here are some things to consider:

- Choose a doctor who has hospital admitting privileges, rather than a tie-in with a mortuary.
- Avoid university physicians with teaching licence to use your body to instruct interns on such procedures as the rectal examination.

There are easier ways to meet people who become intimate at short notice.

- Never choose a family doctor who works with a bunch of other doctors in a clinic that has only one waiting room. That waiting room will be crowded with patients, including ricocheting kids, producing a cocktail of infectious diseases guaranteed to send you home with anything from chicken pox to leprosy, regardless of whether you've already had it.

- In the doctor's waiting room do not sit near, let alone touch, any of the plague-ridden magazines. The elderly *National Geographic* will merely deepen the depression of the patient too sick to travel. As will the *Reader's Digest* with print large enough to be read by a bat at one hundred yards. Remember that the older doctor has traded the Hippocratic oath for swearing at the government. Declare yourself an anarchist. Avoid any political small talk that may trigger the doctor's ranting at the country's ruling party — especially during a colonoscopy.

The routine way for the doctor to get rid of the older patient is to send him or her to a *specialist*. Not only is there an excellent chance that the patient will hop the twig before he can get an appointment with the specialist, but the specialist will define particular reasons to hate the government.

The Specialist

Surviving the specialist can take a lot out of an elderly person. With rare exceptions, it is an ordeal that makes the Spanish Inquisition look like a game of twenty questions.

For starters, the specialist discounts all the information that your family doctor has sweated out of you. Your name, your age, your gender, your symptoms: all under suspicion.

The specialist produces a virgin sheet of paper and takes your "history." If you aren't already history, the specialist will document it. Nothing is too irrelevant to escape the specialist's pen.

"Have children run in your family?" … "Do you feel that your knee has been affected by your marriage?" … "How long have you had that nervous twitch in your left eye?"

The specialist then produces a clay model of a normal knee, hip, or whatever is giving you hell, and quickly details why *your* knee, hip, or whatever bears no resemblance. You nod like a bobble-head doll and already regret prying into your physical condition.

Then the specialist — just to give your anxiety attack a booster shot — propels you into his *examining room*. This is a closet with pretensions. So confining that intimacy is unavoidable.

"Take off all your clothes," says the specialist, "except your socks."

The specialist then goes out. Leaves you alone to hurriedly strip down to the only garment that does nothing for decency. Your socks. One of which has sprung a hole, under pressure from the toes that curled during the interview.

The specialist is gone for quite a while.

Sitting naked as sin on the examining bench, you have ample time to speculate about the circumstances or events that may have prevented his returning during your lifetime. The building, for instance, may be on fire. Or the specialist's wife may have phoned to say that she is leaving him to live with another specialist. Or the specialist may simply have forgotten where he put you, in the excitement of his coffee break.

You toy with the idea of putting at least your pants back on. No, the specialist may return suddenly and catch you defying an order. God is not to be mocked, and neither is the proctologist.

You may also be tempted to try to catch a nap on the examining bench. Not feasible. That bench in every doctor's office is the most inhospitable piece of furniture ever to come out of the Middle Ages. Too high, too narrow, too hard, too much resemblance to a bier in a Gothic Irish church. For the older patient, climbing onto that thing presents the same challenge as Everest. But without the backup from the Sherpas.

Also, to protect it from the patient's bodily fluids, the bench is swathed in a sheet of the most slippery paper ever born of ancient China. To describe it as unstable is like calling Emperor Nero morally challenged. The only relatively safe way to mount this vaulting block is to be lowered onto it by forkli—

But the specialist returns. Scaring you onto the bench regardless of osteoarthritis. And leaving you ready to confess to medical conditions totally unrelated to why you came to this place. If your problem is shoulder pain, the specialist will feel you up and ask: "Why is one of your legs shorter than the other?"

"Pardon? One of my legs is shorter than the other?"

"Certainly. You can see for yourself. You must have trouble pedalling a bike."

Thanks to this tendency of medical specialists to be more interested in your irrelevant afflictions than in that which put you in this mortifying situation, the allotted time runs out.

"Okay, you can get dressed." The specialist leaves the examining room, keeping his conclusions confidential. His report will go on file in your family doctor's office, to supplement a lifetime of similar unread reports, X-rays, C-scans, and MRIs. Modelled after FBI files on foreign agents, the patient's record is a triumph of secrecy. Over your dead body: that is the criterion for release of any of this investigation into your physical states.

Thus the old person may have to wait till he's dead to find out what killed him. Obituaries do fill a gap.

Other Predators on Old Folk

The medical specialist is not the only hazard in the path of the elderly. Other nefarious predators:

The Fly Snatcher

This sneaky menace — never caught in the act — unzips your fly in situations where gappy pants are not appropriate. Wedding parties. Court appearances.

The funeral of a loved one who can no longer see an open fly as inviting.

Because the Fly Snatcher avoids detection, younger people blame the evidence on the older person's failing attention to detail before leaving the bathroom. The unsecured slacks are seen as a symptom of galloping senility. Reason enough to pop Grandpa into the nursing home, before he forgets to put on his pants entirely.

On the older woman, her slacks' open fly may be mistaken for a fashion statement. The Fly Snatcher therefore rarely chooses her for prey, but works almost exclusively in the area around men's room urinals.

The Print Shrink

The Print Shrink attacks the visual field of seniors, reducing the size of lettering on warning signs for which your eyeglasses were not formulated. For example, the door sign "WOMEN" becomes "FOR MEN."

The Print Shrink also plays its tricks on the Internet, so that an innocent old gentleman may be caught watching a porn channel, simply because the Print Shrink has messed with the menu.

Typographers scoff at the idea of a Print Shrink, accusing us of foolish pride, combined with being too cheap to buy glasses with lenses. Humbug! All of us have had print shrink and disappear before our very eyes, especially in letters from creditors or relatives seeking cash loans.

The Whiffle

Habitat: golf courses. Shaped like a three iron. When the elderly golfer drives his ball off the tee, the Whiffle instantly catches it in mid-air and, lightning quick, returns the ball to the tee before the golfer has even finished his swing.

So fast is the Whiffle that the old golfer's companions may accuse him of having missed the ball altogether. This can lead to acrimonious debate and possibly bloodshed.

Unfortunately the Whiffle is too swift about its wicked business for anyone to catch it, let alone to learn how it tastes barbecued.

This bird is responsible for more bad language (including profanity) than any other flyer except a Mexican airline.

The Gurk

Peculiar to the tidal waters of the bathtub. Often confused with a rubber duckie or impaired bathing cap, the Gurk waits till the elderly bather fumbles the soap, then dives to the bottom and hides the soap someplace where the bather will not find it till he steps on it.

The Gurk is responsible for countless broken hips every year, as well as the proliferation of soap-on-a-rope as a birthday present.

The Muffled Phart

For older persons whose diet consists mostly of baked beans, the Muffled Phart is an insidious rider of the wind. A single specimen of this menace can ruin a church baptism, a Christmas family reunion, or indeed any assembly not held on the Galapagos Islands.

The Shoelace Shrike

Deadly to any old person who ventures out of his slippers, the Shoelace Shrike swoops out of the closet and tugs the laces untied. It then hides and warbles "Yoo-hoo!" provocatively so that the old person trips over his laces in his haste to respond. This is why women mostly outlive men: shoes without laces.

The Hair and Now

After age sixty-five your hair stops growing where you want it and starts sprouting in places where you don't.

The most obvious area struck by alopecia is, of course, the scalp. One day a person makes the mistake of looking in the mirror and sees it: the *bald spot*. A sneaky apparition, this, at the top rear of the head, where it may remain unnoticed for years, except by persons who might otherwise have been interested in the front of the head. As well as in other parts of the body where hair remains abundant if superfluous.

This non-cranial hair — which has the consistency and charm of baling wire — sprouts as eyebrows, nostril turf, and ear weed. It is the toughest fibre known to man. It defies ordinary nail clippers. For arthritic fingers — already trembling from an abortive attempt to pare a toenail (the *second* toughest material) — deadly peril lies in trying to prune the barbed brow clutching at your eyeball. No insurance company will cover it.

As for that bald spot, it grows nothing but bigger, and the older man seeking romance with a younger woman must understand that sooner or later he is going to have to take off his hat. Also that very few sex partners yearn to run their fingers through your alopecia.

On the plus side, baldness has been connoted as an indicator of virility, a theory supported by no medical research whatever.

Regardless, many professional basketball and football players shave their scalps, presumably to reduce wind resistance. The youthful role model is there, for the older guy who opts for the depilated pate as more maintenance-free than trying to comb those pathetic few remaining strands over the wasteland.

Despite these heroic measures, for many seniors intimacy is restricted to the rendezvous with their barber or hairdresser, who will profitably spend a lot of time snapping scissors on thin air. The sound is comforting to the customer (the Samson syndrome).

The barber's main function, however, is to tailor conversation. Many elderly persons suffer from live-voice deprival. For one reason or another, other people — family members, for instance — have stopped communicating with the person in the chair, except by e-mail or mental telepathy. And, being fully bibbed, the oldster feels free to spill his guts.

Like taxi drivers, barbers and hair stylists — out of the kindness of their tip — are skilled at fashioning conversation. If a senior can't afford a psychiatrist, his next best audience is the barber. Who also makes you smell better. An added dimension to Pope's "Rape of the Lock."

The alternative to enriching a hairdresser is of course to wear a hat. The senior doesn't need to be an orthodox Jew to wear a hat for most occasions. He could be on his way to or from the Calgary Stampede, where the Stetson is not only de rigueur but a place to carry one's lunch.

Driving into the Sunset

The automobile is a friendly environment for the elderly, because none of the mirrors are set to reflect the driver's face. A woman may use the rear-view mirror to check her lipstick, and be appalled enough to total a cyclist, but an old man can drive a car for years without observing any signs of aging or road construction.

To an old lady an automobile is just transportation, but to an old man his car is a refuge from reality, right up to the moment his alter ego has an interview with a fire hydrant.

His car is the only place where he can still put his foot down and watch people jump.

However, the elderly do need to take certain precautions, if they have reason to believe that the car they are driving is in motion. For instance, the oldster should always wear a hat while driving. Reason: if other drivers see your grey hair, they immediately know (for sure) that:

- you are blind in one eye and can't see out the other,
- you have the reflexes of a spastic turnip,
- you fear going to Hell for exceeding the speed limit, and
- your hearing is such as to interpret being honked at as a compliment.

In the event of a collision with another vehicle (including semis, trains, and aircraft), any driver over sixty-five is automatically held to be 120 percent responsible.

It doesn't matter that the other driver admits that he was the one who drove through the red light or may have been distracted by the blonde on his lap. The cops will give you a Breathalyzer test that detects a percentage of Geritol in the blood. And the paramedics will commiserate with the other driver, even as they load you into the ambulance. And if the case goes to court, the judge will ignore the other evidence, being satisfied that your advanced age caused the collision, even though your car was parked in your driveway at the time.

True, the older driver can't turn his head as quickly as before his neck lost its pivot. Or, having turned it too fast, he may have trouble resuming attention to the road. Or parking in any space smaller than North America. Curbs, in particular, become very aggressive as drivers get older. A curb will veer, suddenly, from its normal place parallel to the street, and attack a tire with a screech heard for blocks.

It is a fact that most accidents involving seniors occur in supermarket parking lots. Whose parking spaces have been cunningly designed by agents of auto-body repair shops to eventually produce the maximum of dings.

Grandpa or Grandma can also get into trouble operating a loaded basket, with a good chance of having to be rushed to Emergency with a celery stalk up the nose.

Our Old Pal Pain

Pain results from a part of our body trying to tell us something, too late. Old people tolerate pain better than young people, because having *no* pain means that part of our body has said, "The hell with it."

Younger people like to think that for old people pain doesn't hurt as much. They assume that we keep a stiff upper lip because our dentures don't fit. Well, that may be a contributing factor. But the main reasons why the elderly are not observed rolling about on the floor, moaning with pain, are:

1. It hurts to get down on the floor.
2. We may never get up from the floor.
3. The floor has just been cleaned and we're not allowed to lie on it.

The old person is subject to *relative* pain (a pain in the ass), usually a nephew.

Because pain is such an integral part of the lifestyle of seniors, much of their attention is focused on *painkillers*. The cause of the pain is something that they try to avoid looking into, in case they find out and create a headache, which is the only pain they don't already have.

This is why drug manufacturers prosper even if the rest of the economy is treading water in the toilet. And their relentless research proves that Ponce de Leon was right: the Fountain of Youth will be found in North America. Probably somewhere near Trenton, New Jersey.

Their new drugs have names easier to pronounce than acetylsalicylic acid, which is contraindicated because a person can sprain his tongue trying to say it. Better known as Aspirin, this painkiller remains popular despite some evidence that, if consumed by the handful, it can turn the stomach into a volleyball.

This feature explains the popularity of *acetaminophen*, a.k.a. Tylenol, which is easier to say without inducing potentially fatal hiccups.

The main hazards for seniors taking any of these painkillers — whether regular, extra-strength, or bye-bye bowel — are:

1.   remembering to take the drug,
2.   remembering that you have taken the drug, and
3.   remembering 911.

One way to keep track of self-medication: immediately after rising in the morning, line up all of the pill bottles on the *left-hand* side of the bathroom sink, and as you take each drug during the day, place the bottle on the *right-hand* side of the sink. This method assumes that you have your own sink. If you share a sink with a spouse or domestic pet, you may be retiring at night satisfied that you have swallowed your partner's corn remover.

There is of course no practical way of remembering to take a drug that must be kept refrigerated. The Post-It Note on the fridge door has a lifespan of about twenty minutes. The senior is wise to avoid pain whose remedy can't be kept at room temperature.

By far the most popular pain among the elderly is of course that caused by *osteoarthritis*. The name comes from the Greek words *osteo*, for bone, and *arthron*, for joint. That nearly all of us have to deal with a bone in a Greek joint is just more evidence that life is unfair even to people who have worked to keep fit. The lifelong couch potato has the last laugh, though it is interrupted by smoker's cough.

The ways of dealing with arthritic pain vary from never getting out of bed, even at gun point, to never getting into bed, especially for sex. (The missionary position is no longer feasible, for the lay.)

The desperation measure is of course the cortisone shot. Doctors are reluctant to administer this quick and inexpensive treatment because it is quick and inexpensive. They may point out that it will need to be repeated, possibly before you can get out of their office

Down Memory Lane Without a Map

Short-term memory loss. This is another thing we older folk have to cope with. Luckily most of us don't remember that we have it. What we have instead is *long-term* memory. We have a clear recollection of everything that happened before 1950. Some of us even clearly remember details of the Second World War. The latrine detail, for instance. We may have forgotten to flush the toilet this morning, but we can dig you a field privy to specifications.

Seniors have not really benefited much from the medical research that has identified the part of the brain that is wired for short-term memory. All we actually know about it is that it is lined with rubber, so that even important messages and directives — e.g., remember to put the seat down — bounce off to the detriment of personal safety.

There are several ways of treating short-term memory loss …

Okay, so they are not easy to remember.

One thing we should try hard to remember, though, is the names of people to whom we have just been formally introduced, as recently as five minutes ago. Also, there is not a chance in hell of your remembering the following ways of compensating for short-term memory loss ...

Okay, so I found the notes.

1. Write reminder notes to yourself. (Carry a pencil in your teeth if necessary. If you write nothing but e-mail, you may let the whole world know that you need to pick up more Metamucil.)

2. Leave your reminder note in a place where you are likely to find it in your lifetime. Taped to the door of the liquor cabinet is good. Or the telly screen.

3. Never use initials or abbreviations in a reminder note ("Phone W. today!" or "Repair broken glb!") Exasperation is doubled by failing to remember what a reminder note was alerting us not to forget.

4. Forget about tying a string around your finger. Not only is this a physical impossibility, but it will mean nothing after five minutes.

How effective are the products alleged to reduce loss of short-term memory? No one seems to remember. However, most of these memory boosters are Chinese herbs called by unusual names like ginseng, ginko, gunko, or something else that starts with a "g." The new, robust economy of China is built on the export to the West of these wonder weeds. Which are sold at natural food stores at prices that are a shock treatment for the buyer, who experiences an immediate, miraculous recovery in his ability to remember his bank account balance.

Another popular remedy for short-term memory loss is chocolate. Chocolate, being 110 percent sugar, causes the brain to light up like Times Square. There is no clinical evidence that chocolate benefits memory, but who cares?

Certainly not the French, who have a phrase — "l'esprit de l'escalier" — staircase wit, meaning the snappy rejoinder that comes to mind too late. Old people have this facility, as well as "mattress memory," or remembering what you were supposed to do before you went to bed. The horizontal position encourages blood to access the brain. Result: the senior may have to go to bed three or four times before finally retiring for the night, or till the next pee, whichever comes first.

Short-term memory loss is sometimes confused with *absent-mindedness*, which is not confined to university professors. It has been proven that the mind is not actually absent, in profs, but is preoccupied with matters beyond the ken of mere mortals. Old persons may make the same claim, so long as they wear a jacket with leather patches at the elbow. They can then worry less about forgetting to turn off the stove or putting the cat in the fridge.

Forgetting people's names can be more serious, especially if the names include your own. Every oldster should start the day by asking the mirror, "What's your name, bunky?" If your reflection just stares back blankly, go back to bed and try again later.

Remembering the names of family members is simplified by calling everyone "dear" or "love." These sobriquets do imply affection, but not enough to incite sexual arousal, in, say, the letter carrier.

Some names the senior must — even if it means writing the name on his hand — remember, including those of:

- his doctor,
- his priest (or golf pro), and
- his auto mechanic.

Calling any of these "Pootsie" can jeopardize his or her usefulness in extending one's life. Yet one should avoid the overkill of addressing the maitre d' or customs officer as "Excellency." Sarcasm is readily assumed, in today's touchy society. And one can never go too far wrong with "Guv" or "Ma'am," so long as the addressee is a biped.

Pros and Constipation

At sixty-five, people stop caring about the relative strength of the toilet paper they use. They are just happy to need to use anything that folds. Reason: *lazy bowels*. In fact the whole digestive tract becomes indolent. It has been working for years at waste disposal, having to deal with garbage left outside by the stomach, one of the least environmentally friendly organs in the entire body.

Also, though the oldster may have shortened in height, he or she still has over thirty feet of guts — far more than we need to deal with the Arrowroot cookie and cup of tea. We are not eating our ancestor's extra helping of buffalo, horns included. Our tripe is just storing natural gas, which will escape, under sudden pressure, at a time when the social atmosphere does not benefit.

Because of a Western diet that is low on roughage such as tree bark and hard-backed insects, we are subject to what may be called the "American Constipation." Whose dictates include:

- If you haven't gone for a week, see a doctor.
- If you haven't gone for two weeks, get a second opinion.
- If you haven't gone for three weeks, inform your next of kin.
- If you haven't gone for a month, call Ripley.

The reality is: if life is a symphony, you've heard the last movement.

The health books that constitute most of our home library assure us that occasional constipation is no cause for alarm, that it is normal for older folk to go for days — or rather not go for days — without having occasion to put the toilet seat down unless mandated by gender.

We are also reminded that our constipation helps to relieve the city's sewage disposal problem. Or adds to the longevity of the septic tank. Think *positive*, they tell us, about not contributing to the pollution of the Earth's oceans.

Still, we tend to fret. After a month or so of this public service, we panic. Even that doesn't help. Nothing. Nada. And so we open the chamber that houses our arsenal — to use the word dangerously — of laxatives. These range from nuclear weapons (castor oil) to brews whipped up by witches under contract to U.S. pharmaceuticals.

The mega-bomb: Metamucil. This bulk carrier is taken with enough water to float the Canadian Navy. It is wise to cancel all social engagements for three days subsequent to taking Metamucil. Some people even join a religious order that requires sequestration.

Others — hooked on human society — will try to relieve the rectal log jam by pushing not only fluids but every fruit reputed to have purgative virtues. One tries to learn to love *prunes*. Not an easy exercise, especially when one is subject to wrinkles oneself. And apples. One of which a day is reputed to keep the doctor of internal medicine away.

We are also urged to eat the skin of all this fruit, including pineapple. "Peel me a grape," though sexy, is contraindicated for the constipated.

Nuts are good, especially if eaten unshelled. As is pasture grass. (How often do you see a constipated cow?)

Par for the Intercourse

Geriatric sex. At what age is a person considered to be too old to qualify? Some observers believe that the sexual-activity span may be equated to the speed limits for motorists (in miles per hour):

- thirty-five is the norm, in urban areas
- sixty-five (with frequent stops for overheating)
- ninety (unsafe in any condition)

Some gerontologists believe that sex for the elderly is the same as in youth except that everything is done in very slow motion. If you have ever observed a three-toed sloth climbing a tree branch, you have a guide to the pace of senescent foreplay. (Which is not just a matter of yelling "Fore!" before falling into the bed.)

What is better documented is that certain variations of sexual intercourse are not realistic for the elderly person wishing to avoid awkward explanation to the paramedics. For instance, the celebrated "69" conjunction is revised to "911." Handcuffs should not be applied unless the aging lover has first posted a note, in clear sight, as to the locaton of the key.

And aphrodisiac drugs, such as gin, should be taken only internally.

Medical literature on the subject suggests that sex is less important to women after menopause than it is for guys, who refuse to read it as a pause for men. The enormous commercial success of Viagra — the libido additive for lads — indicates that, for a significantly high percentage of males, the march of Time has trodden on their most vital appendage.

The medical term for the malady is *erectile dysfunction*. ED for short. ED occurs when sexual attraction fails to be an elevating experience. The blood — which in youth was Johnny-on-the-spot at the least visual, tactile, or olfactory stimulus — now does its unfunny impersonation of a puddle. The spirit is willing, the flesh is not too weak, but the juice is stalled in the "Off" position.

Besides the replacement of Lourdes by Viagra — which is now heralded on ballpark billboards where Bovril once reigned — medical science offers a number of mechanical devices that don't depend on the presence of an attractive female, but will work just as well near a standard lamp. These include a pump, somewhat like a bicycle pump, and various other contraptions designed to get the blood off its ass.

None of these, unfortunately, comes with a warranty, and any may be difficult to explain to airport security inspecting luggage.

All these aids to conjunction in the twilight years encounter a sad truth: after age fifty, most women would sooner settle for a hug. A warm hug, certainly. Maybe even including a kiss that doesn't get out of hand, or a hand that stays within bounds. But nothing that requires removal of clothing, let alone buying a bearskin rug.

It is the old guys who refuse to admit that the thirty-two positions have taken a cut down to about 0.5, give or take a decimal.

Even a standard kiss on the mouth can be hazardous, if it moves you off your cane.

What is *definitely* not a good way of showing your affection is putting your tongue in your partner's ear. Chances are, she or he is wearing a battery-operated hearing aid. The contact of a wet tongue can not only short this sensitive device but fuse the tongue to an expensive item, resulting in another embarrassing episode with the paramedics.

What *is* recommended for the old guy wanting to display affection: a kiss on the palm of the hand.

Her hand, that is. The palm is surprisingly sensitive. And of course gentlemen of all ages have for centuries been kissing a lady's hand as a romantic gesture that also establishes that she is not holding a knife.

If the gentleman is a hygiene freak who is reluctant to kiss a lady's hand unless he knows where she's been, he may have a problem. The old person should understand that sexual intercourse is, after all, only one element of a loving relationship. If it has been 99 percent, he has a bigger problem.

And trying to solve it by getting a dog from the SPCA is just going to spell trouble for the pooch.

The Second (Who's Counting?) Career

"It's better to wear out than rust out." This adage, which has never been thoroughly tested for logic, nevertheless has appeal for seniors compulsorily retired at sixty-five. Their resistance to being reduced to vegetable status is encouraged by the fact that most jobs no longer require physical strength.

If your breath shows up on a mirror, you're qualified.

The senior can move mountains, if lifted into the seat of a bulldozer.

No, it may not be realistic for an eighty-year-old man to get a job waiting tables at Hooters, but Tim Hortons is hiring.

Also encouraging: the oldest worker in America is one hundred years young and still ambling to the office. He is living and probably breathing evidence of the demographics that show that the smaller families fostered by baby boomers have inverted the pyramid of working population. The mummy is still working, and daddy gets offers.

Why? Because the older person possesses an invaluable asset: *experience*. At first glance, the self-assessing senior may judge that all his experience has been bad, and therefore of no commercial value. Wrong! Even if he or she has spent most of his or her life in jail, the old con may find clientele as an incarceration consultant. Charging university researchers big bucks to document the effects of compulsory confinement on the reproductive system.

Other advantages that the older person has as a job-seeker: most jobs today are sedentary. And sitting is what a senior does best, after lying. He is unlikely to leave his desk for any reason other than to go to the bathroom, where he gets his most creative ideas. The senior, being devoid of ambition, is no threat to his or her employer, unless the employer is even older. If too senile to get a job in a business office, the senior can always run for *political* office. He has learned how to deal with warring factions (his family) and is not encumbered with ideals.

Many seniors find a satisfying second career in becoming a professional *protester*. There is never a shortage of public issues — national or local — that invite protest. And protesting is an excellent way of getting seen on TV — albeit in a panorama shot — just by holding a placard and looking militant. Protesting keeps a senior *proactive*, often in company with younger people of the opposite sex. The adrenaline gets pumped, and if this results in a fatal heart attack, what better way to go than in battle?

The senior's menu of protest is ample: same-sex marriage or any other union activity. Any change in the city's public transit system based solely on efficiency. Introduction of slot machines in nursing homes. Shock treatment of the cod industry. Surveillance cameras in the liquor stores.

Note: tree-hugging is a bit dicey for the senior protester, and in fact chaining yourself to *anything* is not worth the risk of being ignored and possibly getting eaten by ants.

On the other hand, confining your protesting to writing letters to the editor of the local newspaper does nothing for your social life and can aggravate sexual impotence if none of your letters are printed.

Green Thumbing

Okay, you have reached the age when the only thing you can realistically imagine bedding is a rose bush. Even this modest intercourse depends on the senior's living in a place blessed with a garden. (Being limited to a window box in a high-rise is not going to exercise the large muscles, or get you emotionally involved with slug bait.)

The plus side of gardening includes:

1. Planting a tree in your garden is a kind of legacy, something that will make you feel better about having nothing else to leave to posterity. A tree assures that younger members of the family will think of you every time they have to rake leaves. And you will have earned the gratitude of a lot of birds in need of a place to poop.

2. Think shrubs. These can prove handy when the older guy is caught short while working in the garden. They should be acid-loving plants, other than cactus.

3. Even though all your garden plants die in a matter of hours after planting, there is a certain amount of satisfaction in your being predeceased.

Other virtues of senile horticulture:

Old wives appreciate the garden as a place to park the old husband. It "gets him out of the house" — a proven air conditioner.

Also, gardening qualifies as *physical exercise*, though done in slow motion. Just *tottering* around the garden, making mental notes of jobs to be done at a future date, helps to slow the hardening of such arteries as are still open.

But the most rewarding feature of the senior's gardening is that it affords an opportunity to talk to complete strangers, *en passant*, without the addictive hazards of the Internet. (Chatlines can become a rubber crutch for the older chatter.) But exchanging pleasantries with someone whose dog has just defecated on your boulevard is relatively innocuous. And if you don't have a boulevard, the city is now creating street-intersection kiosks where nearby residents may do sociable gardening in conjunction with getting creamed by a delivery truck.

Gardening hazards besides the sand trap:

After sixty-five, a person should break off his relationship with a lawn. Smart seniors move into condos or townhouses where the lawn is not only postage-stamp size but is tended by a communal grass-cutter who has no emotional involvement with the fescue. Yet many seniors stubbornly hold onto their detached dwelling with its even more detached lawn. A grave — as in Forest Lawn — mistake.

Why? *Because grass has no respect for old people.* Despite being repeatedly mowed and severely spoken to, a lawn goes right on growing and developing illicit relationships with buttercups, clover, and even *crab-grass*. Which have caused terminal hypertension in more seniors than has any other living organism outside the family.

Instead of being hag-ridden by a lawn, the senior is smart to have it replaced with a *rock garden*. The beauty of rocks is that:

- Rocks don't grow on you.
- Rocks don't develop exotic diseases that require the expensive services of a rock therapist whose bill suggests that you should never have expanded beyond the rocks in your head.
- While diamonds are a girl's best friend, other rocks are a wiser choice for old guys.

However, even the grassless gardener faces certain hazards that might have been avoided if he or she had chosen some motionless activity, such as running for political office. For example, with his notoriously bad back, the senior who gardens vigorously risks spending the rest of his life as a lawn gnome, sullied by bird poop and beyond hope of chiropractic.

A lesser liability: the gardening senior — having long since lost his gloves — suffers from chronically dirty nails. Not only fingernails but also toenails, though how soil is transmitted through orthopedic boots is one of the mysteries of life when prolonged.

Another phenomenon: *old fingernails cannot be cleaned*. The grime has bonded with tissue, to defy excavation and destroy any hope of dating a manicurist.

This Augean condition of old fingernails — which compound the problem by being the only part of the body that grows inches overnight — contributes to the general impression that the old person has become *unhygienic*. And should be institutionalized before he lowers property values in the neighbourhood.

This is why the gardening senior should wear gloves at all times, indoors and out. They go with the territory.

The Hell of Gates

Question: How does the old fogey deal with the personal computer? Answer: Don't *let* the computer get personal. Deal with it at arm's length. Try not to be in the same room with the damned thing, unless accompanied by a teenager.

Reason: The chances are that anyone now over sixty-five did not attend a school where the bullies included the class computer. He got nothing on-line but washed socks. The only virus he had to worry about was the head cold, which didn't wipe out his memory unless he over-medicated with hot toddies.

For those of us now seniors there was little chance of our stumbling upon pornography. We had to go looking for it. As the man said: we didn't even own a pornograph.

Today, there's a pornograph right in your grandchild's room. No wonder the kid goes to school sleepy: he's been up all night circumventing the screen his parents put on the Net smut.

In contrast, Grandpa does not adapt well to the chatlines. He trusts the human voice: that vanishing species of personal communication. His hand shakes too much for him to turn his message over to a mouse.

On the plus side, the older user does gain a new relationship. With his or her computer repairman. Not only are they are on a first-name basis but the technician's emergency phone number is right up there on the board with 911. They may exchange Christmas cards, and it is not unusual for a senior to ask his computer guy to approve his choice of new drapes.

Constant exposure to e-mail addresses can make an already bewildered mind forget what capital letters are for. The Supreme Being becomes god.com. Who defers to Dave, at Technologic Inc.

When the codger's computer "crashes" — a daily event as dependable as rain in Rupert — Dave is summoned to arrange the conveyance of the stricken computer to the Higher Power, which is located in Texas. The cost of resurrection wipes out any capital the owner has left.

On the plus side, long after the old person's own memory has "crashed," the computer may be counted on to remember *everything*, if booted in the right place. Can't, for the moment, recall your spouse's name? No problem. Just log on to "Helpmate." And there it is — "Sears."

But the main hazard presented by e-mail is that of creating personal correspondence with someone in a remote part of the world where human sacrifice is still in vogue. The old, lonely person is susceptible to becoming very intimate with an electronic pen pal who may or may not be collecting body parts for a private experiment.

E-mailed photographs are not to be trusted. The picture may have been taken thirty years ago. Like the one *you* are e-mailing.

Also, though it is possible for parents to vaccinate their child's computer against porn channels — which by all accounts have the largest voyeuring audience since Rome's Colosseum orgies were cancelled because of an outbreak of Germanic tribes — what if it is Grandpa who blunders into the Web site of Spiderwoman? She who feasts on the flies of men's pants? The effect could easily cancel out the benefit of his blood pressure medication. True, he would die with a grin on his face (*risus erectus*), but his obituary notice would have to be evasive about cause of death.

The computer has thus raised the age limit for being the victim of Temptation. Being confined to bed, even, does not spare the senior from what the laptop offers in the way of vices formerly restricted to the young but now available to Grandma, regardless of whether she has been around the block more times than a FedEx truck.

Finally, the Net enmeshes old folks who are too frail to go shopping in person. Their son or daughter may be the last to know that their inheritance has been blown on a partnership in owning a ski lodge in Cuba.

The bottom line: the isolating of the elderly has been one of the larger mistakes of Western society. It set old folks free to get into all sorts of trouble that they would not have had time for if they had to wait to use the bathroom, or the computer.

Too Personal Hygiene

After age sixty-five, the most dangerous room in the house is the bathroom. There can be no doubt that the older person would live a lot longer if she — and especially he — never went to the bathroom. For anything. Yes, it would put a strain on the kitchen sink, but the medieval system of sanitation — dumping the contents of the commode out the window to the street below — had a lot to be said for it, though not by passersby.

Modern plumbing has created most of the hazards for the elderly:

The bathtub

Statistically the source of at least 60 percent of the income of orthopedic surgeons doing hip replacements. Driven by fear of being identified as a malodorous source of air pollution, the oldster wobbles into that trough of scalding water without a life preserver. Bad knees make lowering the body a major project, involving grab bars, a Goodyear no-skid, all-season bath mat, and blasphemy that compromises divine aid. If the senior settles for a shower, disaster lurks in the soap that escapes the hand, scuttles under the nearest foot, and triggers the demolition that proves that only brides should have showers. (Soap-on-a-rope works well provided that the elderly bather is already planning to hang himself.)

The toilet

Almost as perilous as the tub. Armed with two lids, which may be left up by the old married guy only if he wants to be flayed alive by an irate spouse. The john is the well from Hell. Reason: with the old guy's aging, the short arm loses both aim and velocity. Thus very old men are lumbered with the mantra: sit to be sure. Nothing can be more noxious to a male's self-image than having to adopt the female approach to a pee. He now knows the squat that smarts. And demonstrates that indoor plumbing does more to emasculate men than even daytime televion.

The medicine cabinet/drawer

This storage space is apt to be a massive jumble of little bottles containing prescription drugs dating back to Hippocrates. Plus various nostrums that had their day as wonder drugs and now just make the senior wonder what they were for.

Old guys likely have prehistoric ampoules of ginseng at the back of the drawer, souvenirs of the days when fear of sexual impotence overrode the rent money. Having had time to reroot, the ginseng now just scares the cleaning lady.

On the prescription drugs, the expiry date is now hard to read — 2001? 1901? 1001? — increasing the temptation to throw them out. But no one does.

Another depressant for the old guy is finding the package of condoms long after he becomes aroused by no one but Don Cherry.

The bisexual medicine cabinet is likely to have aged badly because it bulges with a mixture of abandoned medication to:

a) remove hair,
b) restore hair, and
c) grow its own hair.

No question: older couples need to have their own, individual, clearly marked HIS and HER medicine cabinets. They may share the same automobile with relative safety, but community property was never intended to include the toothpaste.

Toilet paper

Despite the lyrical TV commercials, this perverse parchment can wipe out the senior's image of dignity by clinging to the heel of the shoe, unobserved except by the rest of the world. Thus it can be the ruin of a court appearance ... wedding reception ... investiture ceremony, etc. Downy soft though it wasn't, the corncob of our pioneer forefathers was safer than the treacherous teepee.

Other Domestic Death Traps

Statistics show that most accidents occur in the home. This is where children are conceived, usually, resulting in a lot of grief that might have been avoided if you had been a vagrant. And not frequented such dangerous areas as:

1. The kitchen

Assuming, that is, that the kitchen houses a stove (a latent incinerator), also the microwave oven that doubles as a death ray, a drawer full of cutlery (1001 ways to commit harakiri), glassware poised to shatter at a glance, and a closet whose brooms and mops miss no opportunity to snare the slow of foot.

2. The bathroom

When shared, a major cause of divorce. Community property should never include the toothpaste.

3. The basement

The area to which old men go to die. Sometimes from natural causes but more often from letting their mind wander while operating a power tool. This is why there are more widows than widowers: knitting needles do not attack when they smell fear. Denied proper lubrication for forty years, even a lawnmower can turn on an old man and remove an appendage.

4. The linen closet

To the untrained eye, there would appear to be little risk of an old man's being terminated by a linen closet. Yet it happens all the time. The victim is just reaching in for a clean towel and *whoosh* — he gets buried under an avalanche of toilet paper rolls. An ugly way to go. Snowy but sad. Cause of death never mentioned in the obituary notice. Thus it is not generally recognized that the home linen closet houses a mountain range of white stuff that can become unstable. Especially if the old guy is likewise.

5. The attic

This walk-in cloister affords special opportunity for a life-shortening concussion. Old people have inevitably, over a lifetime, used the attic to store a wide variety of objects that bear a grudge for being crowded into an unheated loft. If *we* were that carton of mentally disturbed income tax records, we too would miss no chance to trip the owner into sharp contact with a naked beam. Even if the oldster wears a hard hat to enter his attic, the detritus of memorabilia will remind him that he is not only over the hill but losing his brakes. Add the risk of being attacked by a mad bat, and the attic is seen to be a lethal chamber to be avoided.

6. Stairs

These are the reason why, when you complain to your doctor about your naggy knees, he or she says, "Sell your house." So you move into a ground-level apartment and contract terminal mildew.

These adjustments are facilitated by advice from your *environmental therapist*. This is a nice person who comes to your home and identifies all the hazards whose removal, collectively, will cost you the arm and leg that are already heavily mortgaged. In the bathroom alone, the environmental therapist spots dozens of perils to life and limb, recreating a simple launch into the tub as fraught with its own Scylla and Charybdis.

The therapist prescribes grab bars on the tub, a non-skid bath stool, an ejection seat on the toilet, plus removal of the bathroom's lush carpet of mould on all fixtures, including possibly the owner. It may be necessary to bring in a jackhammer and an accredited demolition expert.

After paying for all these improvements to his home environment, the senior may find that he has less need for the bathroom because he can't afford food. And is too weak from hunger to use the enhanced stairs. Everything conspires to confine him to his bed, which is a safe place only till forces disguised as family invade to turn his mattress.

You may even die in your own bed — an offence against the billion-dollar medicare system that depends largely on your dying in a hospital or other government-approved facility.

So, do the right thing. Crawl out of bed despite hurting. Go to the environmentally friendly bathroom. And absently take the wrong medication.

We owe it to the system.

When the Eyes Don't Have It

It's a fact: unlike French wines, your eyes don't improve with age. The first mistake was opening your eyes, as a newborn, and exposing them to the glare of your father's grin. From the crib on, it's all downhill, visually speaking.

What was saucy winking in high school becomes a spastic twitch, subject to misinterpretation by a police officer.

Then, around fifty or so, we notice that newsprint has shrunk badly, though the paper hasn't got wet. The publisher economizing on ink? Possibly, but just to check, we make our first visit to an *optometrist*. Who proves to be no relation to an optimist.

The optometrist tests our ability to read a chart of letters of the alphabet that puts a severe demand on our ability to guess correctly. He then sells us our first pair of glasses, designed to be shatter-proof when we look at the optometrist's bill. Today's eyeglasses are much smaller and lighter than the spectacles our grandparents wore. This makes them easier to lose till you sit on them. A person is likely to sit on several pairs of glasses before he graduates to the office of the *ophthalmologist*.

Everyone dreads going to the ophthalmologist because the word is impossible to say unless one has a natural lisp. Yet his or her waiting room is apt to be crowded with old folk whose winks are no longer voluntary.

The ophthalmologist shines an intense blue light into your eyeball and finds that you have no soul. But what he reports is that the pressure on your optic nerve is roughly equivalent to that on the Cleveland Dam. If you don't already have glaucoma, you can expect it to kick in before you get back to your car.

Alternatively, the eye doctor tells you, "You have a cataract in that eye."

A cataract? You knew your eye was watery, but this is ridiculous.

The eye doctor patiently explains that your eyeball has clouded over, with the threat of precipitation in the form of tears. Luckily there are new kinds of eye drops that reduce the pressure on everything but the wallet.

In the land of the blind, the one-eyed man is king, but he still has trouble finding proper sunglasses. Which the older person should wear even when he is not having to make a court appearance. One benefit: sunglasses help to conceal ogling. An old guy wearing shades can stand on a street corner, treating his optic nerve to a parade of snug jeans, without drawing scorn. If he wants to hold a tin cup at the same time, he can pick up enough change to pay for the glasses.

Hear, Hear!

The benefits of sunglasses — and indeed all types of spectacles except the pince-nez — depend on a person's having ears. Without ears, the glasses would, sooner or later, slide off the end of our nose. Possibly resulting in a six-car pileup.

This is why having ears is important, even to seniors who feel that they have heard everything.

Unfortunately, ear maintenance can be even more expensive than conserving sight. The ears' owner should understand that old ears have a function other than growing hedge to screen out sound. They should still be an aid to *hearing*. Cupping the ear with the hand, as a hearing aid, is now seen as a sign of poor financial circumstances, inviting the scorn of head waiters and realtors alike.

Nor does just nodding the head serve as a viable substitute for hearing, outside the home. Appearing to be in agreement can have bad consequences, especially in a pub.

The ear trumpet having lost favour in our youth-oriented culture, the oldster is apt to be exposed to an *audiologist*, the most expensive ear accessory short of a diamond stud.

The odd thing about the audiologist's prescribed hearing aid is that — unlike buying an automobile, for instance — the smaller the device, the more it costs. (For some reason, being partly deaf bears more social stigma than being hard of sight.) Thus the most expensive hearing aid — operated by the tiniest, teentsiest battery known to man — fits snugly into the earhole. If someone whispers sweet nothings into that ear, it can fry your brain.

With his or her ear costing an arm and a leg and the nose bearing a small fortune in magnifying glass, the elderly person's head now consumes more of the pension and RRIF than any other part of the body. Everything below the neck is relatively disadvantaged, not to say destitute. This seems unfair, since the lower body has, over a lifetime, provided a lot more fun than the appendage that wears a hat.

The Mature Driver Inquisition

One good reason to live in an anarchic society, such as the Congo or Paris, France, is that bailiwicks like ours require a complete medical examination of drivers over eighty. The prime of life!

About 40 percent of drivers opt to surrender their licence, rather than flunk the mature driver's medical. This is deplorable, a bad example to younger drivers. It is much gutsier to keep taking the medical test till you find a doctor who will accept a bribe.

So, it is never too soon to plan a strategy to prevent one's being ruthlessly divested of one's wheels, if these are connected to an engine. For the medical exam, choose a doctor who may take a liberal view of your test results. Note: An old doctor cannot be trusted to identify with your vital need to drive your car. It is smarter to find a young doctor who is trying to build a clientele and is more likely to respond to your plea that you need your car *in order to drive to the doctor's office*. (Cab allergy.)

For your eye test, try to persuade the doctor to place the letters chart a reasonable distance away (twelve inches), and ignore the smaller letters in favour of those large enough to be read by a senior on another planet. Don't be afraid to guess what each letter is. Boldly stating that the V is a U may make the doctor momentarily doubt his own sight.

Self-confidence is also essential in order to pass the next test of your ability to drive in traffic: blood pressure. When we are young, no one cares a fig about our blood pressure. Our blood is assumed to be under no pressure whatever. It just burbles along, singing a song, ignoring gravity and other sad sacks. We can *blush*, whether we want to or not. And the cheeks are not the only parts of the body to get suffused at the drop of a hint. Our blood is agurgle with good attitude.

But the instant we turn sixty-five — wham! The pressure is on. Our blood gets *hypertensive*, unable to relax and enjoy just cruising along the veins and arteries, occasionally dropping in on the heart to get pumped. Instead, the blood bums around, mainlining *cholesterol*. This is a mysterious substance derived from any human food that is tasty. That is *bad* cholesterol. Good cholesterol is found only in fish with no criminal record. It is to measure his *bad* cholesterol that the doctor sends the senior to a *medical lab*, where all the blood's dirty little secrets are documented.

The medical lab is a good place to meet other people who have the same interest, namely getting the hell out of there. The downside is that the lab blabs a blood reading that proves, beyond reasonable doubt, that consuming too many doughnuts is going to put you on the bus. If not a hearse. Or, at a minimum, if the lab's report doesn't make your doctor cross himself and utter a profanity, you have seen your last pizza.

To try to avoid another ugly scene with their family physician, many people check on their blood pressure with the machine provided gratis at their pharmacy. If you resort to this sneaky strategy, *don't tell your doctor*. It will only make *his* blood pressure go up. You don't want his resultant death riding along on your other guilt trips.

Duds for the Doddery

Clothes make the man, but only up to age sixty-five. After that, clothes throw in the towel. Which looks even worse on the old guy.

Women continue to buy new clothes for themselves long after their body has lost interest. A woman wants to be buried in something nice. A guy settles for clean underwear. (He may ask to be cremated in his wedding suit, just to get even.)

Old ladies still enjoy tottering into a dress shop, even if only to browse. But elderly gentlemen are found wandering in the mall only if they have become severely disoriented while looking for the liquor store. A partial list of clothes to avoid:

- Bermuda shorts that have shrunk around the Azores,
- high heels (especially on old guys), and
- anything low-cut, form-fitting, or revealing more than the basic signs of life.

Old men suffer from clothestrophobia, or fear of store changing rooms. Being confined in one of those oubliettes, alone with a pair of new trousers whose legs just won't quit, and a salesperson loitering outside ready to call 911, an old man is subject to a panic attack that results in his zippering up more pubic hair than is consistent with a comfortable fit.

He buys only orthopedic shoes. With tread tested by Firestone. To oblige his gimpy knees and back, he also buys so many cushioning insoles for the shoes that he stands considerably higher than when he entered the store, and may require oxygen.

Getting fitted with this footwear by a female clerk may be the extent of his sex life. But being approached by a male clerk may alarm him, if already doubting his sexual orientation, and trigger a hasty retreat from the shoe store. Old ladies are spared this angst, viewing the female clerk as purely functional.

They are also less likely to advertise to the assembled company that they have a hole in their sock. That is the old guy's forte. The removal of his shoe is the occasion for the big toe to make a sensational, show-stopping appearance — ta-da! Betrayed by his socks, the shopper loses the last vestige of the Cinderella story. He is ready to take any shoe, regardless of size or fit, just to get that damned exhibitionist digit off the public stage.

Having learned a hard lesson, the old man buys no other clothes for the rest of his life. Besides, he has closets full of jackets, pants, and coats he never wears, never will wear again, yet hates to offer to a charity in case they are rejected.

The average older man also owns roughly 350 kippered neckties, including the snap-on bowtie that has often fallen off to provide comic relief on formal occasions. The old school tie has graduated to moth fodder. And in his bureau drawer molders a mass of detritus including:

- several pairs of Charlie Chaplin gloves (blown fingers),
- a compass that confirms that he has gone south,
- a Laocoon group of belts and suspenders, and
- the graduation gown that is the last vestige of an education.

Dressing Tips for the Tottery

Is it really necessary for you to get dressed every morning? Unless you plan to go to a wedding or the bank, staying in your nightwear can avoid a variety of accidents, some of them fatal. (Note: Pajamas, whose bottoms are treacherous unless severely belted, are really the young person's bed wear. The nightshirt is a simpler garment to operate. Especially when one is responding to the yell of nature, in the bathroom. A senior may have some aesthetic objection to the nightgown as being redolent of Marley's ghost. But this drawback is more than offset by the freedom from buttons and drawcord that complicate both investiture and divestment. And if you happen to die in your sleep, you are pre-shrouded — a thoughtful touch.)

If you must put on laced shoes, knotting the laces is the most critical phase of the operation. Shoelaces seize every opportunity to slither out of the bind. Then, while attempting perambulation, you step on your own shoelace and — hello, Houston, we have liftoff!

High heels should *definitely* be retired to the shoe rack. Especially by old guys. Yes, even old ladies will be loath to surrender their feet to sensible shoes. But their stilettos will excite arousal only in resident corns and bunions.

As for the other end of the body: the best cure for baldness is a hat. In earlier, more civilized times, wearing a hat was socially mandatory, for both men and women, unless they had good reason to believe that they were indoors. The Queen of England would be unable to go to the Ascot racetrack if she didn't wear a hat — a different hat for each race.

The downside of hat-wearing is that the hat is one more thing to forget if the wearer has taken it off. Every bordello in Nevada has a vast collection of men's hats, abandoned as a result of hasty departure.

Many old guys opt to wear a sweater that is a turtleneck to hide their turkey-neck. This fools nobody, including turtles. But the sweater does obviate the need to wear a necktie, something the senior does only at gun-point. This despite his owning a rackful of enough cravats to hang the entire prison population of China.

The pre-tied bow tie identifies the senior as a retired bartender or barber, an image suggesting manual dexterity but also expectation of getting a tip.

The Out Back

It's a fact: dogs and cats age much better than humans, because they don't develop our back problems. And why is that? *Because Rover and Tiddles are not bipeds*. But people *do* walk upright, putting additional strain on the *spine*, a shish kebab of bones never designed to operate vertical to the ground, which of course it is the minute we make the mistake of getting out of bed.

This is where the great apes, loping along on their knuckles, have the last laugh on evolution, or would have if they weren't subject to becoming extinct because of human poachers. Who deserve all the lumbago they get.

Thus, old humans suffer the ills created by a lifetime of standing more or less erect, often with the additional weight of a blown tire, a fat bride, or other heavy object. Socially, their back is the only part of them that goes out.

(In Australia, the outback is a largely inaccessible area devoid of life. The description fits most seniors' dorsal area.)

The problems created by being erect — not to be confused with those of the more youthful erection that caused a whole different kind of comeuppance — are aggravated by a condition called *arthritis*. Sometimes pronounced "arthuritis." (Arthuritis is confined to Camelot, of course, whereas arthritis besets millions regardless of whether their table is round.)

Arthritis is what causes an old person to walk like a setsquare. Or makes him appear to be about to leap at something — knees bent, eyes bulging, mouth muttering a blasphemous commentary.

Arthritis is what happens when two bones have joint custody of a leg, arm, finger, or any other part of the body where movement was once an option. (Bowel movement doesn't count.) When it is the spine that has become arthritic, even the Quebec separatist movement is a pain in the rear. Finding a place to sit is a standing problem. The victim thinks of Heaven as a place with lots and lots of chairs.

On the plus side, arthritis is the most popular disease in America, with a new diagnosis every thirty-three seconds. Since misery loves company, the senior with arthritis has the comfort of knowing that it is the commonest chronic disease for people over forty-five and therefore much more tolerable than having, say, leprosy.

See Naples and Diet

In fact *all* Italian food is hazardous to an aging digestive system. The fully loaded pizza that was once consumed without qualm has become a land mine that blows the senior's cholesterol level right off the chart. Only the suicidal contemplate cheesecake.

All others observe the following dietary regime:

1. Don't eat anything that isn't dead yet. While seafood is recommended as part of a meatless diet, a senior should not take on a lobster that is not certified deceased. Even consuming raw oysters — always a hazard in the tremulous hand — is doubly dangerous, especially when being slurped in conjunction with a high-calorie blonde.

2. Remember that the latest research into diet factors indicates that a well-balanced meal includes food with the wine. Seniors tend to forget this, because their appetite is not as sharp as it was when they got some exercise besides pulling the chair to the dining table. They come to interpret a three-course meal as (a) the sherry aperitif, (b) the full-bodied burgundy, and (c) the congenial, postprandial brandy. Supplemented with a bowl of mixed nuts. (While nuts are an excellent source of tooth decay, they are short on *protein*, something that even old people need in order to remain a living organism.)

3. Fat *is* beautiful. While younger folk age visibly as a result of their tireless search for the no-fat yogourt, the low-fat celery, and the maybe-just-a-smidgeon-of-fat butter, the senior knows that without fat *food has no flavour*. And since taste is the only one of the five senses left for a senior to enjoy while sober, he can still dream of a life without ketchup.

4. "No sugar added." There's another label blurb that the oldster may cheerfully ignore. Chances are, our sweet tooth is the only dental feature remaining in the mouth that lives for chocolate. Our

idea of a varied diet is to put brown
sugar instead of white on our Jello.

Because in today's society both members of an adult
couple often work at full-time jobs, extra pressure is
put on Grandma to provide the family meal that is
attended by all the family rather than a haggard
quorum. Next to McDonald's, Grandma is the main
resource for cooked food, including takeout.

Some grandmas profess to *enjoy* preparing these
family feeding frenzies, even though there is some
evidence that being expected to lay on a banquet
every Easter, Thanksgiving, Christmas, and family-
member birthday does shorten their life by up to ten
years. Grandma gets a sense of still being needed,
whereas Grandpa is just reminded of how many of
his kin owe him money.

For the old person living alone, the nuisance of
preparing food may be eliminated by Meals On
Wheels, the delivery of nourishment by a volunteer
who owns an automobile and is trying to compensate
for a lifetime of sin. To qualify for this service the
senior must exhibit a convincing degree of physical
or mental incapacity. Just jumping nimbly into bed as
the wheeled meal is arriving may not suffice.
Especially if there is someone already in the bed.

The Needs of Knees

In youth, we take our knees for granted. We can kneel, for God's sake, or on weekdays. Without the kind of planning that went into D-Day.

Then, we could actually cross our knees. Now our knees cross us. Uncrossing them may require professional assistance. These knees betray us if we attempt genuflection, devout or lay. Squatting is visionary. Or permanent. The knees dictate.

Staircases, in particular, are hostile to old knees. Despite the double hand rails that are mandatory in the homes of the elderly, ascending or descending cannot be achieved without putting some pressure on the knees, which is why we worship Otis, God of Elevators.

For old knees, walking *up* stairs is not as hazardous as going down. The stairway to Heaven looks less formidable than the steps in the other direction, without an escalator. Wealthy knees may be able to afford the installation of a funicular, but Groucho Marx always viewed his with suspicion.

Old knees are heard but not seen. The owners avoid wearing shorts because the visual effect can spook the family dog, or be a factor in the wilting of house plants.

The standard treatments for fossilized knees are:

1. Topical analgesic creams, made from chili peppers, that cremate all sensation.
2. Knee replacement, an operation that may need to be repeated if the surgeon is having to support an ex-wife.

Most family physicians, whose gross income is affected by the loss of a patient, are reluctant to recommend the latter unless the patient has actually crawled into their office on all fours. Or the patient's moaning is loud enough to disturb other patients in the waiting room.

Instead, the doctor first shows the patient various exercises designed to stiffen the upper lip. This type of treatment is called *physiotherapy*, a method pioneered by the Marquis de Sade. It creates a physical ordeal that makes the original knee pain seem trivial.

Most physiotherapists are young women who are much stronger than they look and demand that the male patient remove his pants before they examine his knee. This panics the patient who is unsure of the state of his underwear, and may lead to further knee damage when he scrambles to get a pant leg over a shoe.

Another unnerving element of physio is *acupuncture*. Acupuncture was created by the same folks that invented the Death of a Thousand Cuts. In the hands of a motivated woman — possibly abused as a child by an older man — acupuncture shows how far the fair sex has moved away from traditional needlework.

How acupuncture works is not clearly understood, except that the patient feels less pain when the needles are taken out.

Pain does not return till the patient pays the bill. This indicates that physiotherapy, as a miracle cure, is more expensive than a one-time visit to Lourdes.

Heroic Measures

When physiotherapy, combined with prayer, fails to mitigate the knee pain, the owner may turn to non-prescription drugs that his physician does not recommend because they are available without a doctor's prescription.

These drugs, derived from the sex glands of shellfish that don't have knees but make good money, are supposed to rebuild knee cartilage by means of wishful thinking. How the active ingredient (seaweed) is transformed into human tissue is a mystery whose solution nobody really gives a damn about.

All that is known for sure is that the pills have to be enormous, so that swallowing one requires the gullet of a pelican.

These pills are not taken with food, because nobody can afford to eat after paying for them. Alleged knee restorers like glucosamine are best taken with a cheap white wine till the oldster feels no knee pain, though he is unable to stand up.

The next step up, in extending pain from the knees to the area of the wallet, is *viscosupplementation*. This treatment is believed to intimidate the knee by sheer volume of syllables. Yet viscowhatever is basically nothing but a lube job. Instead of it being your car's suspension that gets a shot of grease, it's your knee that is up on the hoist. It costs about six hundred dollars per shot more, but you don't need to leave your leg in the shop overnight.

These injections serve as a shock absorber, till you get the final bill.

The main advantage of the knee greasing: it can be done in the doctor's office, which is insulated so that screams cannot be heard by patients in the waiting room.

If a person is willing to go public with his bad knee, he may submit it to *arthroscopic surgery*. Which involves quite a crowd of spectators, even in a private hospital.

Knee scoping is so popular that there is a waiting list to get on the waiting list. Which is shorter in the U.S., but the knee costs an arm and a leg.

Assuming that the candidate lives long enough to be scheduled for vacuuming, he can expect to be called suddenly into a hospital bed, where his knee immediately stops hurting. For the first time in years. Too late! The nurse orders him to remove all his clothes, in full view of the other patients in the ward, who are grateful for the good laugh.

"Do you want to watch the operation on the monitor?"

Since there is no extra charge for this opportunity to watch a horror show starring our knee, most of us say "Sure!"

Wrong answer.

This author made the mistake of being unable to resist a freebie, with no commercials.

Among the printable observations:

1. Before the operation, the anesthetist offers a choice of ways to avoid the discomfort of having your knee dredged: gas, spinal injection, or a bullet to bite on. This patient chose the needle. Another mistake. Losing all feeling below the waist eliminates the option of jumping off the gurney, screaming, "I've changed my mind!"

2. Lying flat on your back with your head swivelled for half an hour to stare at a monitor puts a severe strain on the entertainment value of the show. Yet it's less disturbing than looking at the faces of the orderlies and nurses also watching your knee being sucked clean of garbage. The masks don't conceal the revulsion. You can see them mentally swearing off contact sports, snowboarding, Latin dances ...

3. In terms of bodily evacuation, having your knee scoped is not as exhilarating as giving birth to a baby. No cigar.

Gramping and Granny Knots

One way that a grandparent may total his or her knee
is by dandling a toddler on it. Today's toddler can
weigh up to fifty pounds. The old person would as lief
dandle a Buick. Especially if the child is subject to
motion sickness. But dandling grandchildren seems
to be a tradition, one that makes Christmas more
physically hazardous than just erecting the tree.

Thus the only safe posture for a grandparent at a
festive family occasion is to lie on the floor, in the
fetal position.

One of the tenets of family life is that, as the
grandparent gets older, he or she enters a second
childhood — i.e., becomes slightly daft — and oper-
ates on the same primitive level, mentally and physically, as a three-year-old grandchild. Because both
generations share urinary incontinence, other family
members assume that they may be suitably isolated in
another room, or county.

Also, the grandparent is seen as a built-in
babysitter. Unpaid, of course. It is conservatively
estimated that if a grandparent were paid the going
rate for a warranted babysitter ($30 an hour, plus

tip) grandparents, as a class, would be the wealthiest persons in the Western world.

Another phenomenon of today's society is the evolution of the single mom into the *single grannie*. And — somewhat more exotic — the single grandpa. Other distinguishing features:

- The single grannie wears spike heels with cornplaster toes.
- She knows what men want without their having to fill out a questionnaire.
- With regard to practising safe sex:
  - she doesn't need the practice,
  - he doesn't need the safe, and
  - both consider sex without love to be a viable alternative.

This freedom may be seriously impaired by adult children who, because of failed marriage, loss of employment, addiction to illegal substance, etc., return to the family home for shelter. This is why it is not uncommon to see an older guy hammering a "FOR SALE" sign into the front lawn of the family home. Often only minutes after his son's or daughter's wedding reception has broken up. It's insurance against the return of the native.

Grandparents who *really* want to chicken out on family responsibilities will opt for joining a retirement community well away from schools and shopping malls, often supplemented with a golf course where every hole is a par twenty. Here relatives may expect to be greeted with barbed wire and guard dogs. It's a place where the grandparents may live happily ever after, or till the bank shreds their credit cards, whichever comes first.

Pets for the Mature Masochist

Very often the senior has lost the marriage partner, as a result of death, divorce, or simply leaving the spouse alone in a wilderness area. Most commonly it is the wife who is now a widow and needing something to clean up after. This is why we see so many old ladies out walking small, short-hair male dogs on a leash. They are compensating for the lost hubby, but with a companion that doesn't shed or leave the seat up.

There is controversy over whether, with time, a person's dog comes to resemble the owner, or the other way around. What *is* demonstrable is that the larger the widow, the smaller the dog. In contrast, old men prefer to be seen with a big dog, in case the promenade turns violent. But the pet's food bill deters most seniors from owning a mastiff, let alone a horse.

For the lone senior who is allergic to the outdoors the ideal companion is of course a cat. A cat doesn't need to be walked, getting plenty of exercise climbing curtains or going on long, territorial hikes that strengthen the owner's relationship with the SPCA. The only other caveat with a cat is that the cat has never got over being considered sacred by the ancient Egyptians. Thus the senior must accept the feline's viewing him or her as a potential human sacrifice. It is one way for a person to feel wanted, though less so than a pound of liver.

As for supporting a parrot as a pet, only the wealthy senior can afford the cost of even a previously owned bird. Which may also have an intimidating vocabulary ("Eff off, matey!") unsuitable for visitors and some family members.

A canary is a more practical pet, especially if you are living in a coal mine, or other social housing. A budgie, however, can be a major disappointment when you realize that it is not normal for the bird to sleep on its back.

What about a poisonous snake? A great conversation piece, winning respect from neighbours, but hard to kennel. Also, you have to suspect the motive of the family member who surprises you with the Christmas gift of a boa constrictor.

As for other reptiles, such as turtles or tortoises, disappointment lies in expecting to have a pet that moves more slowly than you do. A motivated turtle can hustle its hump at a surprising pace, so that the senior joins the hare in being humbled by a shellful of wrinkles.

Finally, there are fish. The home aquarium is perfect for the senior who wants a pet that is likely to predecease him. The average domestic goldfish has a life expectancy of about two hours, or as long as needed to fetch it from the pet shop, whichever comes first.

It may be possible to become emotionally attached to a goldfish, but it will have to be a rush job.

The point is: everyone — and this includes older folk — needs to feel needed by some living entity as a reason to get out of bed in the morning. Unless a person has led an entirely self-centred life, she or he has to water something, clean its litter box, or just talk to the rubber plant about its for God's sake shaping up.

Problems with the Plumbing

Old men spend much of their remaining years in the bathroom gazing at a urinary trickle that, as spectacle, is no competition for Niagara Falls.

If pressure was a problem in the past — at the office, say — there is none now in the john. Tinkling into the toilet is a gravity feed only. An elderly male astronaut would be in big trouble.

On the plus side, the danger of overshooting — one of the hazards of youth — has been replaced by that of no projection at all. A peril to pants; a menace to cleaning ladies.

Older women have their own special problem: bladder control in conditions that induce laughter. (The easiest way to intimidate an old witch, if encountered, is to tickle her.) But at least old ladies are spared the humiliation of having to cozy up to the public urinal beside some kid who is nailing it from feet away.

The old guy prefers to wait for a cubicle, despite drawing suspicion as some kind of pervert. This is why he avoids public concerts, fitness centers, jury duty ...

Such waning of the wee-wee is usually attributable to BPH (benign prostatic hypertrophy), the condition where the prostate gland, having nothing better to do, starts to crowd and bully the bladder duct. New drugs dealing with BPH have proved to have highly beneficial effects on the revenue of drug manufacturers.

One school of thought — a school where recess is the main program — cites the unproven theory that ejaculating regularly (two to three times per week) will prevent prostate enlargement. "There is no scientific proof or this," says this authority, "but it is risk-free." This assertion is suspect. Having sex on medical grounds may not meet the criteria of a guy's partner, even if she is a professional nurse.

"I need to bang you tonight, dear. Just to boost the old tinkle, eh?"

Lots of luck!

As for solitary masturbation, even as a BPH-preventative measure, the treatment is clouded by the biblical injunction (no spilling seed upon the ground), though the operation is done indoors.

To alleviate the BPH symptom of having to get up from bed several times a night just to pee, so that your bathroom window smacks of lighthouse to the neighbours, the doctor may suggest *sitting* on the toilet. "Like a woman," he says. This is supposed to help the bladder empty more fully than if a guy is standing, kneeling, or tapdancing.

Achtung! Squatting on the john like a woman can affect a man's self-esteem. If he is already sensitive to being judged as a bit effeminate — because he shaves his legs or listens to CBC Radio — this micturating posture may aggravate his neurosis. In rare cases the side effects include his being unable to pass a dress shop.

Raising the toilet seat may be an old man's only remaining uplifting experience. Sitting on it, for other than evacuation number two, is a demeaning reminder that Rodin never did a sculpture titled *The Tinkler*.

In any event, once it's enlarged, the only reliable way to deal with the prostate — which already caused a lot of trouble by being confused with the prostrate — is by having an operation called transurethral prostatic resection. A Tupper to its friends. What was once the Crown Jewels is now Tupperware.

"The urologist reams it out," your doctor informs you, thus creating your self-image as a clogged drain.

Some BPH victims balk at the Tupper, fearing that the laser will hang a left and render them impotent. They fear this even though they are already impotent. They don't want to be more impotent. They have laid in a lifetime supply of Viagra and don't want that investment compromised by botched surgery.

Such is the fantasy. The fact: for most men over seventy, an erection is a Japanese election.

Jockey shorts that once appeared to bear a cucumber now manifest a gherkin. Just *seeing* a jockey, let alone the horse, has a depressing effect that discourages old men from going to the racetrack. Visually, bingo is more benign.

The geezers take the loss of libido more reluctantly than do old gals, most of whom seem actually relieved to get the Godzilla-sized monkey off their back. They act as though there are other things in life more important than sex. Once they definitely stop producing eggs, they lose interest in the whole dairy business. The old rooster, however, clings to the illusion that he can still be the cock of the walk, with a little help from his pharmacist.

For very wealthy old men, the anti-impotence device of choice is attachment to a young, beautiful blonde. Who knows which side her bed is bettered on. However, the success of this treatment is often clouded by the intervention of a fatal heart attack. Which is of course every man's dream — pole-vaulting into Paradise. But most older men are too wedded to reality and a mortgage to be able to follow the Hugh Hefner route to Heaven.

Getting the Finger

The best evidence that God is female is that only men — especially dirty old men — get a rectal examination. The reasons given for this mortifying procedure are that:

1. men have the prostate gland, and
2. having assisted in the pleasurable process of procreation, this gland avenges a lot of women by developing ailments that make a man hate his entire pubic housing.

A lot of mystery surrounds the rectal examination of the prostate gland. Most men haven't even heard of this degrading rite of passage till it's too late. Informed earlier in life, most would elect to live dangerously — as a stunt pilot or a department store complaints manager — rather than live long enough to have to submit to a rectal.

For one thing, it's a rear entrance. Your mother told you to beware such access in a lower-class neighbourhood. Right, Mom.

Next, when a motorist gives you the finger, he is using the same digit employed by the doctor to invade your privacy. This is why male drivers resent The Finger more than women drivers do. The Finger has this special, and humiliating, connotation for a guy.

Hence the importance, when a guy is choosing a doctor, of his sizing up the MD's hands. Nice, dainty, feminine hands are a wise choice. Beware the paw whose digit has the potential of taking a turn for the wurst. And projecting the patient on a flight some-where north of the moon.

The choice of suicide is made even easier if the guy's doctor is a woman. Who tells him to curl up, pants and undershorts down, on a bench, in the fetal position, to await the insertion of The Finger From Hell. Which probes. God, does it probe! For lumps. A lumpy prostate, according to recent research, is not desirable.

But the doctor never tells you whether the finger has struck gold or not. Instead he or she hastily strips off the rubber glove and tosses it in the garbage. If he or she then sprays the garbage with the fire extin-guisher and rushes it out of the building, you know you have a problem.

To Sleep, Perchance to Snore

Some older couples still sleep in the same bed. It helps to keep down the heating bill.

Only the affluent have separate bedrooms. Hopefully in the same house or apartment. But if two old folks *are* still sharing the same bed, probably one of them is dead. Or neither of them snores.

Their growing resemblance to a dyspeptic turkey may be related to the custom of going to bed at dusk and getting up at dawn. The senior crawls into the sack earlier and earlier, till he starts to fear the dark. He may take his favourite golf club to bed with him to fend off the forces of darkness.

But the oldster has a harder time getting embraced in the arms of Morpheus. Morph prefers kids. We may feel that the old god of dreams should be hugging a person his own age. But the senior has to take a number.

It is an oddity of aging that the mind that was idling while the owner was more or less vertical lays rubber when he lies down with the intention of losing consciousness. Insomnia. Not the high-grade wakefulness of the young, worrying about school exams or an unexpected pregnancy, but *nitpicky* thoughts.

Like, why does my pillow feel abnormally lumpy tonight? Or, did I remember to remove my denture, and if not whose teeth are those grinning at me? Or, hey, my knees really don't like each other!

Various devices are prescribed to overcome sleep resistance:

- **Sex.** ("Excuse me, dear, but may we screw so that I can get some sleep?") Wrong motivation. May result in being suddenly rendered unconscious — not the best type of shut-eye.

- **Counting Sheep.** Highly overrated. Not everyone can think like a border collie — a very alert canine. And a ram can turn nasty if he thinks you're messing with his flock.
- **Music.** Listening to the radio station's golden oldies of the fifties and sixties can be counter-productive if Frank Sinatra reminds you of the affair you had in New York, with someone who proved disloyal after you left the hotel elevator. Listen to ultra-lite opera.
- **Drugs.** Should be the last resort for sleep, but are usually the first. Since sleeping pills present an in-house invitation to overdose, a sedative drug should be kept locked in a safe. By the time the old person remembers the combination, she or he will have fallen asleep.

The Nappy Gaffer

Although the senior may get only eight hours of sleep a night, she or especially he will compensate by falling asleep during the day — in a chair, at church, watching curling on TV…

When planned, this daytime dormancy is called "a nap" (beneficial), as opposed to the more spontaneous "dozing off" (inappropriate when in company, driving a car, or operating power tools).

Some Latin peoples, such as the Mexicans, have institutionalized the nap as the siesta. These sensible folk make full use of the sombrero, which is large enough to cover the face and make it difficult for others (including relatives) to tell whether they are meditating, snoozing, or dead.

Some old folk have mastered the art of napping with their eyes open. Many of these learned the skill while serving at various levels of government, or on university senates. (The suspicion that some senior higher court judges have had their eyelids surgically removed is probably unfounded, and it is perhaps unwise for a grandparent to fool around with toothpicks, just to appear to be awake watching the school concert.)

In the event that the old person does fall asleep in bed, the biggest change he notices is in the quality of his dreams. The old guy is likely not subject to the mixed blessing of the "wet" dream. The well has gone dry, so Jack and Jill have no incentive to get it on.

Instead, the elderly are subject to *nightmares* that can draw on a lifetime of hairy episodes stored in memory. Sweet dreams have been largely replaced by those lower in sucrose, higher in saturated fits.

Teeth — True or False?

After sixty-five, the only oral exam you have to pass is that given by your dentist. Chances are, your dentist represents one of your longer lasting relationships. Wives and husbands come and go, in today's society, but the person in the white smock has been taking care of your disposable income longer than the tax department.

We should, of course, have taken better care of our teeth ourselves, since they have been more or less permanent residents of our mouth. But of all our sins, the failure to floss, and floss more regularly than just before we visited the dentist, costs us the most pain in Hell's class comeuppance.

The senior who has postponed his regular visit to the dentist — and few occasions fail to qualify as a good excuse for doing so (family funeral for a dead goldfish, unfavourable alignment of astral bodies, etc.) — pays the price. And pain is not deductible as a medical expense.

Although the oldster usually welcomes getting a phone call from *anybody*, he or she makes an exception when the caller is the dentist's office to remind the person that the regular four-month checkup is overdue by several years. Nag, nag, nag!

It is to try to minimize this humbug that the senior buys an expensive electric toothbrush that promises to discourage bacteria by severely agitating the gums. There is no evidence that an electric toothbrush is more effective than an ordinary toothbrush held in a somewhat palsied hand, enhanced by a postprandial brandy. Also better for the hydro bill.

Other seniors succumb to the seductive ads for *teeth whitener*, the promise to restore the smile of youth in a pan of wrinkles. However, the effect of this bleach job may be only scary, startling waiters into dropping trays and causing severe depression in the family cat. Also other family members may be encouraged to wipe the smile off your face.

Instead of resorting to cosmetic overlays, the savvy senior compensates for his incisors by becoming *inscrutable*. Avoid laughing in company. (No need to Scotch-tape the lips together. Instead, think of yourself as a Mona Lisa, whose thin smile has been credited to her having fangs.)

One place where it is especially prudent to keep your mouth shut: the dentist's office. Besides pretending that you are from the mysterious East (Toronto), don't get lured into telling the truth when the dentist asks, "Is that tooth still acting up?"

"No, no!" you say. "It only bothers me if I chew on that side."

That ought to satisfy the busybody holding the record of your chronic lies. But, no. Instead the fusspot writes out a *referral* to another dentist — the one who does the heavy jackhammer work in a soundproof cell.

Performing a root canal

This canal is no Dutch treat, but an excursion into one's capacity to endure extreme pain while listening to classical music.

To delay the ordeal for as long as possible, the thinking senior is alert to warning signs, such as his dentist's crossing himself before looking in your mouth. And he isn't even Catholic.

Another solution — adopt a lifestyle that eliminates natural teeth early on by:

- playing ice hockey,
- dating redheads, and
- living on Oreos.

Then, welcome to the wonderful world of dentures! Partial or complete, here is the prosthesis you can park in a glass of water beside your bed and get smiled upon all night long.

Raising Cane

It's a must. The day that you turn sixty-five, you get a cane. No, not a sugar cane, Dad. Make that clear to relatives buying your birthday present. You want a *real* cane. Not necessarily an alpenstock, but something heavier than a modified putter. It doesn't matter that you can still walk without a cane. Serving as a third lower appendage — alright, Jocko, fourth — is only one of the cane's basic functions.

As a pedestrian, you need your cane to intimidate motorists. That is why ideally it should be a *white* cane. With a soupçon of shillelagh.

So that if a motorist ignores your demand to stop while you totter across the street, you can whack her fender as she roars past. If the driver then stops and appears hostile, you collapse to the road and feign having been struck by the vehicle. A crowd will quickly gather (potential witnesses) and you have the basis for a lawsuit that the motorist will be happy to settle out of court.

As a cane-wielding shopper you get faster service in stores, whose clerks become nervous about the welfare of merchandise — especially crockery or cosmetics — in proximity to someone casting about with a cudgel. The cane may also be used to trip other customers headed for the same product.

With practice, using a cane can actually make a person look jaunty. Gene Kelly and Donald O'Connor did a dance number with canes that should be an inspiration to anyone who also owns a straw hat. The cane owner should, however, practise jauntiness in front of a mirror, lest the gyration be read as a seizure of some kind.

Some people (not many) actually need a cane to help them walk. Bizarre, yes, but not every senior can afford delivered pizza on a daily basis. Yet walking with a cane requires a degree of skill if it is to be an influence on locomotion.

So. Assuming that the cane is long enough to reach the ground, the user should not let his cane become a crutch. That is, the knobby end is held in the hand. Thus a decision must be made: which hand to hold the cane with. If the user has a "bad" leg, it is normal to use the corresponding hand to grip the cane that serves to supplement the "bad" leg. Wrong! The "bad" leg will just get worse if it thinks it can depend on a cane to support the intolerable weight of the body. The cane should move with the "good" leg, as a reward for behaving itself in public.

Finally, whether one carries a cane for show or for blow, the equation for the No. 1 problem is: Cane + Short-term memory loss = Embarrassing scene.

"Hey, you forgot your cane!" This clarion summons, whether shouted by waiter, bus driver, or bank clerk, advertises to the world that a doddery object is on the loose.

This is why the cane should bear one's name, phone number, and e-mail address — if one can remember them. This does not ensure that the finder will return the cane to the owner. Alas, "finders keepers" is the norm for lost canes. A cane is handy for staking a garden shrub, warding off burglars, and, of course, whaling small children who have pinched something you can't use.

So, if the old person is attached to his cane it should be by a chain to the wrist. That may impair some social activities, but the bottom line is: You don't need to be absent-minded to lose your faith in humanity.

Seniors Discounted

Many trades advertise a discount — usually a percentage to be named later, if at all — on alleged work done for seniors. The most obvious exception, on the evidence of the phone book's Yellow Pages: the escort services.

A phone call to Sensual Playmates, for instance, confirms that asking the question — "Do you give a discount for seniors?" — is greeted with an ominous silence, or possibly a giggly snort, indicating that, whatever relief the escort service provides for the senior, it will not be financial.

While this response from the likes of College Girls Escorts (who obviously ought to know better) represents lack of discrimination on the basis of age, it is no victory for the civil rights commission.

Other recreational venues, such as neighbourhood movie houses, do offer an admission price discount for seniors. It is hard to say which is the more dispiriting: to be asked to provide proof of age or not to be asked. A person can age visibly, just documenting his or her antiquity.

The Discount Dracula also lurks in carpet cleaners, who know that seniors are apt to have carpets on which enough stuff has been spilled to turn the Oriental into the downright Byzantine. The rug is probably more animated than the owner. Thus the discount is easily absorbed with the coffee stains, resulting in a tab that proves that it would have been cheaper to have had the rug anesthetized and removed by the SPCA.

A different hazard lurks in the "free delivery" offered to seniors by their neighbourhood supermarket. The wily senior, knowing that the supermarket's parking lot is the optimum site for his becoming roadkill, takes advantage of the "free delivery," and over time develops a special relationship with the free delivery guy, who gradually replaces Santa Claus and family members as a source of caring as well as toilet paper.

Less benign is that seniors get no discount when buying auto insurance. On the contrary, they may be required to pay a premium. As a penalty for not exceeding the speed limit. Elderly drivers — many choosing not to drive at night or in areas frequented by cabs — are rarely responsible for the kind of accident that makes the TV news. Insurance companies love older drivers. Everybody else hates us. No one gives our careful driving a hand. Just the finger.

In short, seniors are discounted on sight. This is why, in the Western world at least, seniors are regarded as discount *people*. And why old people — especially elderly women — spend billions of dollars to avoid looking their age. But the old male is doomed to live out what remains of his life as the Invisible Man. Reduced to clear.

Passing Time Without Straining

Most seniors suffer from an excess of leisure time. After the years of hard work that helped to keep them out of mischief — unless their work was cattle rustling or politics — they suddenly have a lot of time on their hands. And hands sticky with time can pick up undesirable habits, such as watching the neighbours through binoculars or frequenting bingo halls.

The more mind-stimulating pastime is of course *reading*. Novels are not recommended. Especially contemporary novels written by female authors. Such are apt to remind the older reader of how many sexual experiences he or she missed out on because of the earlier social climate. A person used to be able to depend on the public library to screen out material unsuitable for seniors. But no longer. A younger generation of librarians has allowed the shelves to steam visibly with all manner of erotica. The oldster may accidentally pick up a novel that makes Casanova look like Mr. Dressup.

This pretty well boils down seniors' reading to *Reader's Digest*. Which publishes the large-print edition found in doctors' waiting rooms, where it serves as a depressant.

The wealthier senior may subscribe to *National Geographic*, which provides a monthly reminder of all the places in the world that are not wheelchair accessible. This publication, along with others such as *Playboy*, helps to satisfy any masochist streak the geezer may still be harbouring.

As for the daily newspaper that most seniors subscribe to out of habit, the best-read section is the obituaries. It is always a relief not to find one's name there. Also we derive a degree of satisfaction from reading about the lifetime career of someone who died younger than we are. We welcome the fully documented evidence that extraordinary achievement is something that a person pays for with his life. (Okay, so Michelangelo lived to be eighty-nine. He never married.)

Despite the daily newspaper's rarely being a source of intellectual stimulation, reading it is not as totally passive as watching television — today's equivalent to the opium dens of the old Shanghai. Sedentary TV addiction is what makes it difficult for relatives to realize that Grandpa has died, unless he topples out of the chair while watching *Today On Wall Street*.

So, it behooves every senior to spend at least one hour a day doing something less mentally enervating than TV. Watching paint dry, for instance.

Anything but what feeds into the toilet paper commercial that merely adds to depression associated with chronic constipation.

The oldster who is trying to hang onto what are left of his marbles will devote at least part of his waking hours to:

- the daily crossword puzzle,
- a computer chess game, or
- Scrabble, with an opponent under six.

The brain is not a muscle, but it still needs to be exercised to avoid mental avoirdupois (fathead). Just nodding our head, to indicate understanding, will fool people for a time (five minutes), after which it's game over, in terms of being treated as a still-rational human being who just happens to drool a lot.

Finally, retirement — the golden years — is the most popular time to start writing one's autobiography. There is a certain satisfaction in getting our life down on paper, leaving out the bits about contracting a sexually transmitted disease, the arrest on a charge of indecency, and the years spent in a so-called institution. Even though your life story is never published, just the threat of it can be enough to make other family members think twice about beating you up or trying to take away your loaded rifle.

For this project all you need is a good supply of cheap scribblers, lots of pencils with lead in them, and access to the family photo album — plus a few old publicity shots of Gypsy Rose Lee.

Now, the chances of our autobiography being accepted by a publisher other than the vanity press (in which the author pays for the printing plus editorial revisions that affect his blood pressure) are the traditional slim and none. But some member of the family may offer to pay us to burn it. Which is a better deal than hiring a cut-rate literary agent.

How to Addle a Nest Egg

Some people can't wait to turn sixty-five, so they can draw on their pension. If they die at sixty-four, they are really, really pissed off. They have spent all — if not more — of their working life paying into a pension, only to be cheated just because they had a contretemps with a dump truck.

The luckier folk enjoy a brief period (about five minutes) of satisfaction before they learn the difference between living on their pension and continuing to afford food.

The two types of inadequate pension are the Old Age Pension — paid by the government in recognition of not being deceased — and the company pension, which is often heralded by the financial collapse of the private enterprise supposed to pay it.

Both types of pension prove that, as pie in the sky, they have a lot of crust.

To qualify for the OAP, the senior may be required to produce proof of age — a *birth certificate*. Preferably his own. Normally, an elderly person has no recollection of the whereabouts of his birth certificate. It is not a document that he is likely to have framed and put on the mantelpiece. If he has stashed it in a safety deposit box — along with the savings bonds that expired earlier in his life — he must first find the keys to the safety deposit box. At this point his hope of accessing his OAP fades as fast as his blood pressure goes up.

The *company pension* requires less research since it is paid on the basis of years of employment, possibly years of work. (Note: it is harder to draw on a company pension if a person has been self-employed. Some self-employed persons do incorporate themselves, in order to qualify for a pension, but end up hating themselves for never having had a retirement party.)

The company pension may be "indexed for inflation." This means that when the price of meat goes up
a dollar, the pension goes up five cents, a process known
as "getting the index finger."

Indexed or not, government or company, the
pension dooms the recipient to being classed as a
pensioner. A stigma that zaps whatever sex life the
senior has posited.

This is why it is smart never to mention your pension to *anyone*. Especially family members or an attractive younger person you happened to meet on a plane
or in a pub. Keep your OAP a dirty little secret between
you and the Department of Human Resources.

In contrast, you can blab all you want about getting a cheque, in season, from your investment broker. Involvement with the stock market is viewed as a
relatively youthful activity, even though it accelerates
the graying of the hair.

The Irrelativity of Time

In old age, everything takes longer to do than when
your blood was circulating. That vital fluid now tends
to puddle. In youth, we were quick to blush. Now, it
may take up to twenty-four hours, even though everything is going downhill.

Cut yourself shaving on Monday, and you won't bleed till Tuesday. Or notice it till Wednesday.

The watch that the company gave you when you were retired has also stopped working. Too bad, since the battery was a substitute for your pulse.

In our youth, a year is the time frame of eternity. From Christmas to Christmas: forever. Then, in middle age, the months start to accelerate. A week shrinks to three or four days, including weekend. After sixty-five, the passing years become a blur. The calendar sheds months in a blizzard of missed reminders. We have the impression that we get ten phone bills a month, weekly notice of property tax, daily garbage pickup...

You rarely see an old person looking at his or her wristwatch. One reason for this is that he or she has forgotten to put it on. Or the numerals have shrunk after he didn't remember to take the watch off before having a bath. Or the problem may be that, to the senior eye, twelve-thirty looks very much like six o'clock, thus causing confusion between lunch and dinner and probably adding alcohol.

Yet old folks are never late for appointments. Not *having* any appointments helps to preserve this record. The only assignation to be met is the doctor appointment. Having a date with a physician pretty well constitutes the old person's social life. The nuclear family having exploded years ago, the names on his dance card are those of his MD, dentist, ophthalmologist, psychiatrist, physiotherapist, estate lawyer, and — digestive system permitting — pizza delivery guy.

With this array of social contacts available, the senior rarely finds time dragging unless he or she is unusually healthy for her or his age. The reason we see more old ladies out walking their dog instead of their husband: the guy had one medical appointment too many and died of complications.

Pharmacy Phantasies

When someone over sixty-five leaves the house, the chances are 98.6 percent that the person is headed for the drugstore. (The rest of the outings are family-oriented and subject to rescheduling. But we don't mess with London Drugs.)

The oldster knows that the pharmacist is the only protection he has from his doctor. Every prescription is scrutinized by the pharmacist's computer. That computer is a surrogate mother-in-law: forgetting nothing, forgiving nothing, ever ready to divulge your gamy medical history. (The Recording Angel uses your pharmacist's computer as a reference tool.)

The pharmacy computer has to deal with a *prescription*, which is something handwritten by the doctor, on a scrap of paper, in a language that predates the Egyptian hieroglyphics of the Rosetta Stone. The pharmacist is trained to translate and, with luck, understand the scrawl.

But first she tells the customer: "This will take ten or fifteen minutes." She then takes the prescription to another pharmacist, and together they huddle over the papyrus, shaking their heads to indicate that for once your doctor has produced a scribble that — despite years of experience in breaking codes for the Secret Service — they are unable to decipher.

Thus you have plenty of time to lurch around the drugstore, gazing at racks of greeting cards that celebrate occasions that you have little, if any, hope of ever experiencing again: birthday, anniversary, Christmas…. (The sympathy cards are relevant but rarely uplifting.) If you blunder into the aisle of cold and flu remedies, where bleary customers are peering at faint hopes, you may pick up a bug to supplement the malady that inspired your prescription.

The savvy prescription-waiter loiters around the shelf of laxatives, where there is less congestion. And is rewarded eventually by hearing the summons, possibly on loudspeaker: "Mr. Hornby, your Viagra is ready and you should be ashamed of yourself!"

That's the worst-case scenario. Actually, the pharmacist is usually the soul of discretion, manifesting no sign that you are a repulsive object. She may even smile as she hands you the bill that wipes any grin off your face. (One of the wonders of modern medicine is how big a bill they can get into one of those little plastic bags, which also contains a wee phial of the priciest cotton wool ever produced by sheep.)

Some old guys avoid the raised eyebrow by going to a "natural" pharmacy, where it is natural to pay even higher prices for nostrums than at the unnatural pharmacy. Natural pharmacy products — derived from medicinal plants so virile that *they* fertilize the grower — are stored in large, stout glass vessels that would look at home in the lab of Dr. Frankenstein.

From these amphora the weedy elixir of choice is ginseng, a plant with knobby forked roots that resemble the legs of an old guy taking a stance for something to be named later. Ginseng tea is believed to be a panacea capable of curing a person of drinking anything but straight Scotch. It has not been clinically tested on rats because rats can't afford it.

This is the main knock on the natural pharmacy: Can you afford to restore your private parts if they cost an arm and a leg?

For Whom the Siren Wails

The emergency vehicle siren. The most dreaded sound the city offers. The old person who hears that banshee wail thinks immediately: Is the ambulance coming for *me*? Somebodylooked at me and decided I needed immediate attention from medics? I've had a serious accident and no one had the heart to tell me?

Or is it the fire truck? Did I start a fire where it was inappropriate? Like, in my bed?

Few of us can tell the difference between the emergency vehicle that takes you in and the one that puts you out.

Not that it matters. Firemen are trained to deal with people who have dialed 911 without giving the matter serious thought. They don't carry those axes just to chop kindling.

It is normal for the 911 call to attract both fire trucks and ambulances, creating a street drama that pretty well demands that the person who made the call has suffered a life-threatening stroke, or lost a limb to the Weed Eater. Neighbours will be disappointed if you have tied up traffic and created a scene just because you were feeling lonely.

The gurney of a lifetime: that is the fate of him who issues a frivolous summons.

At the other extreme, the old person — especially an old lady — may not call for an emergency vehicle till she has tidied up the house — hobbling around on the broken ankle — and put on something that doesn't show the blood. She bites the bullet when ambulance attendants enter her house without removing their shoes.

On the plus side, arriving at the hospital Emergency by ambulance does speed up the entrance, compared to a person's stumbling in off the street without a proper introduction. Reason: before you can be treated in Emergency you have to be *admitted*.

Admissions date back to the Spanish Inquisition which pioneered the methods of forcing people to confess to sins they hadn't committed. The rack has been replaced by the computer, but the operator is equally ruthless about testing the victim's will to live.

If Emergency is having a busy day — i.e., Monday through Sunday — the wanabee patient is stacked in what is called triage, the French word meaning "makes you three times as old as you were before you came in." Thus, right after a 6.3-grade earthquake is probably a bad time for an old person to have a heart attack. Yes, the excuse is there, but so is the crowd that will leave the senior somewhere out in the Emergency parking lot.

With luck, he or she will be eventually promoted to the part of Emergency known to be frequented by medical personnel. All of whom will studiously avoid the person till it is documented that she or he is not:

- infectious,
- wounded in a shoot-out with police, or
- dead.

If you are cleared as non-toxic, an orderly will escort you to a cot in a sheeted oubliette. The orderly has been trained to be pleasant and reassuring without actually touching the patient, while attaching various monitoring machines whose main purpose is to give the hospital immunity from a lawsuit. The orderly then says: "The doctor will be with you shortly." (If the patient believes this, he is already showing signs of hallucination that may or may not be drug-induced.)

The orderly then closes the sheets around the stall, these not to be flung open till the patient has complied with an order to remove all his clothes. These will be replaced, after a life-threatening struggle, by the hospital gown that is one of the last vestiges of medical care as it was practised in the time of the Aztecs. The gown ties at the back, or might if:

- the strings hadn't been ripped off by a previous berserk mental case,
- the patient had the manual dexterity of Copperfield the magician, or
- the patient had no other life's work.

Whichever, it is inevitable that the patient will find it impossible to walk to the john without mooning staff and other patients, a spectacle suggestive of Banquo's ghost at a frat party.

One of these posterior parades will be for the purpose of tinkling in a small bottle that the patient might have hit if he hadn't forgotten to bring his glasses. Why Emergency is curious about one's urine, when the problem is a sprained knee, is just another of the mysteries created by this hospital facility.

Eventually, and when the patient has resigned himself to never escaping Emergency in his lifetime, the doctor appears. It is normal for the patient to become very emotional at this long-awaited manifestation, kissing the doctor's hand and weeping unashamedly.

The Emergency doctor is usually a *resident*, a younger med graduate who needs the practice of treating expendable people who are an evolutionary step up from rats. You get to learn together. This is why the doctor appears very upbeat about your condition unless he finds out what it is.

Meantime the doctor sends the patient to the X-ray department. Before he makes a judgement about your broken toe, he needs to make sure that your lungs are clear. (This is how old people learn about a problem they didn't know they have. It's right there on the plate.)

Then, relatively suddenly, the patient is discharged. All information goes to the next of kin. Emergency also blabs in its report to the family physician, who prefers not to discuss it because he doesn't trust *anybody*.

The bottom line: the old person should not call Emergency unless he or she is having a really dull day. And wants to meet a lot of people who will get intimate without becoming emotionally involved.

Home to Rust

A *home*. Something the old person dreads being put in. She, or especially he, resolves to use all of his or her remaining strength to hang onto their present home's doorknob, as caring family members try to drag the resident off to the Last Resort.

One of the advantages of a federal penitentiary over a rest home is that the inmate doesn't have to pay for his lodging. And of course there is a good chance that the inmate will one day walk out of the facility. Without being pursued by bloody-minded caregivers.

Running away from home is harder after age ninety. Yet a person will use all his remaining cunning to break out of stir and find his way back to his old home, whose new owner will have to beat him off with a broom.

This happens though the *retirement home* offers luxury incarceration. The elderly resident may even have a clear view of a golf course, used by younger people still able to pick up a golf ball without triggering a Code Red.

Actually life in a nursing home is not as bad as we anticipate, provided that the staff are liberal in administering narcotic tranquilizers. The difference between the outward signs of being senile and being stoned is mercifully slight after age eighty-five. Going to pot is the best trip available.

Still, most elderly people would prefer to die in the comfort of their own home. It is usually a family member who becomes unduly concerned about incompetence, such as the oldster's accusing the letter carrier of being an agent of a Middle Eastern terrorist organization, or Grandpa's trying to prune the cat, or his repeatedly phoning 911 to report a suspicious hydrant.

Sooner or later Gramps must yield to relatives or other picky authorities who insist that he fold his oxygen tent and totter into an institution. Chaining oneself to the bed will not deter grim kin.

So, is the oldster advised to accept his fate graciously? With a smile? "I'll treat this as a new adventure in living! A chance to make new friends! To explore the outer space of my soul!" Hell, no. The conscript should make the family feel as guilty as possible, while having to be physically removed by conservation officers.

You have enough rigid parts without adding the stiff upper lip.

Dumping the Stuff of Life

Every oldster sits amid a lifetime collection of Stuff. And that is its assessed value: stuff. Which the senior may or may not want to fall into the hands of his relatives. Like, a personal diary that they will find to be a book of revelations they could do without.

Remember: you are lucky if even *you* have sentimental value.

So, now is the time, while the senior still has the strength to walk to the garbage can, for him to get rid of those items that may diminish the esteem in which he would prefer to be held — at arm's length.

Such as sex toys. Unless you are a retired police officer, the handcuffs found in your bedside table are going to raise eyebrows at a time when you want the whole face to be committed to expressing grief at your passing. Likewise the whip (unless accompanied by a bona fide horse) and the library of videos with titles like "From Bed to Worse." Bite the bullet. Trash the stash.

Bundled letters from an old flame can burn your image to a crisp. The senior needs to go through every old shoe box to make sure that all hold naught but old shoes. It will be too late to explain to a surviving spouse: "I don't know who that person is in that photo. She just happened to be in bed with me when the picture was taken."

If you have been active in sports other than sex — and it can happen — you have a closet full of antique skis, gutless tennis rackets, ovoid basketballs that you have been reluctant to scrap in case medical science made a breakthrough in rejuvenation... That wooden-shafted putter holds a lot of memories — all bad — yet you don't have the heart to chop its head off for the recycling. Maybe the Elysian Fields have a par four.

Often the old person's collections include several generations of rubbish — war medals, photo albums of people wearing funny swimsuits, a stamp collection of very old issues whose value has not been affected by inflation: they are still worth one cent.

In this regard, the senior should seriously consider incinerating any diary kept over the years, possibly in the hope of being posthumously recognized as the next Samuel Pepys. Pepys wrote his diary *in code*, out of respect for Mrs. Pepys. Chances are, any diary you have been keeping is in plain English (or French in Quebec) and will be readily translated by surviving family members who don't need any additional evidence that Grandpa was a devious old letch.

All of this detritus ought to be donated to the dumpster, but nobody has the nerve. We fear that, though aged ninety-five, we may have a sudden need for that old jockstrap, the stiletto heels, the bottom drawer's yellowing batch of love poems we wrote during our Ovid period....

Yet we should bite the bullet, as well as getting rid of the old .22 that it complemented. Leaving the chore to a spouse or children is inconsiderate, a dreary task that makes them more aware of their own mortality and perhaps starts them drinking if they are not already on the sauce.

The Last Will or Wont

"Everyone ought to have a will." So says that TV commercial for homemade will kits, as endorsed by a young couple prone to morbid thoughts. If we haven't thought about death before, television provides a surefire intimation of mortality.

The two things, someone said, that may not be contemplated, are the sun and one's own hopping the twig. This is why most people avoid looking to their will till surrounded by relatives making the sign of the cross.

It was probably comedian Jack Benny who — when told "You can't take it with you" — said, "Then I'm not going." An admirable resolve, but not in immediate touch with reality.

Having accepted the premise of making a will, a person must avoid the temptation to concentrate on the list of relatives he intends to leave *out* of post-mortem goodies. What one sees as the black sheep of the family may turn out wolf instead of mutton. The wayward son or daughter could contest one's will, a bout as bloody-minded as anything whipped up by WWE. A family feud that makes the Capulets and the Montagues look Little League.

And the Cadillac parked in some lawyer's driveway will be financed by our last wishes.

This is why it is a smart idea for the senior to dispose of his or her personal fortune *before* exiting this vale of tears. True, this requires exquisite timing. Giving your kids most of your money while you have reason to believe that you are still alive also assumes evidence that conditions will not change before next Tuesday at the earliest. It can be embarrassing to have to ask a child to return the cash because your heart problem turned out to be just gas.

"Excuse me for living." No parent or grandparent wants to have to utter those words. Yet the law doesn't allow you to sue the doctor who implied that the wart on your nose was terminal.

Being around to observe the gratitude of your kin is gratifying, in a morbid sort of way. But we can't safely depend on a spirit-of-Christmases-to-come to guide us, like Scrooge, around scenes of our bequeathal. Get those turkeys distributed early, so long as you have a honking big bird stashed in your own freezer.

The repulsive reality is that, though we may have lived alone for years, our making a will can draw a crowd consisting almost entirely of *lawyers*. These buzzards have been circling overhead for some time, before we even identified with carrion. Called "estate lawyers," they make their living from the dead. They speak in grave tones. Just shaking hands with one of them can shrink your life expectancy.

The lawyer's premise, in preparing the will, is that without it your family — including relatives you never knew you had — will be fiercely contesting your last wishes. Long-lost brothers and illegitimate children will crawl out of the weeds to lay the sleeve on the swag. Your will is your last testament as to why you can trust only your dog. Unless of course Rover gets legal representation.

In your will you must name an executor. (Not to be confused with an executioner, though both make a killing.) The executor has the responsibility of fulfilling the terms of the will, regardless of whether you were in your right mind to trust *anybody*.

Often the testator — who sounds like a male body part but is actually the person deceased — will name a relative to be his or her executor. This is a good way to get back at a family member from the grave. Executing a will can take years off the executor's life, being right up there with the Chinese death of a thousand cuts as punishment for being a relative. If your will's executor didn't already hate you before you died, he will wish that you were still alive so that he could kill you.

To avoid this post-mortem resentment, the will-maker may assign the executor job to a *trust company*. This invites the question: how much can you trust a trust company? Most trust companies are agencies of large banks aiming to get larger. To distract attention from this commercial aspect, the trust company officer often speaks with an English accent, like the Queen, if indeed he or she can be induced to speak at all. The trust officer prefers to put everything in writing. For which there is a charge that respects the fact that most of the work was done by his secretary, who has expensive tastes in fur coats.

It is usual for this executor to be paid a fee, to which may be added a tip for grief counselling. The executor's fee being a percentage of the total value of the estate, a trust company loses interest in the will of the poor but honest, preferring that of the rich and confirmed dead.

This is why some people elect to write their will without legal supervision. They disregard the old bromide: the person who acts as his own lawyer has a fool for a client. They are playing hopscotch in a mine field.

For one thing, the testator must be at least twenty-one years of age. It is hard to imagine why a teenager would be concerned about who gets the skateboard, in the event that this method of transportation proves to be inimical to life. But will-making is adults-only entertainment.

Of course the will may be challenged on the grounds that the testator was too old to write anything but a note for the milkman. His loving kin could contest the will on the grounds that dear old Dad was, at the time:

- pissed to the gills,
- senile to the point of idiocy, or
- already dead.

Another hazard of the self-written will: the law requires the signing to be witnessed by two (2) persons who are under some obligation to initial things. And who don't stand, or sit, to take any benefit from the will. This exercise can be a depressing reminder of how few people you know well enough to witness *anything* you've done.

So, the chances are that you will have to hire a lawyer just to find some witnesses — usually his secretary, or somebody passing through the office on other business. As a solemn occasion, the whole thing is ruined by a plague of initials. So, you might as well have a lawyer prepare the will in the first place. That is how the law works: eventually you must hire a lawyer, if you are drawing up anything but your socks.

The lawyer keeps a copy of your will, because after you die you will have difficulty finding a copy of the will yourself. Also you need to keep your will in a place where your family, if any, will find it after it becomes evident that you have gone to your reward, if a reward was offered.

Taping your will to the fridge door seems like a good idea, in terms of quick discovery by relatives, but nobody wants to be reminded of his mortality every time he fetches forth a Fudgcicle. A bank safety deposit box is the usual repository for one's will — out of sight and mind, and the charge is tax deductible. The only problem: where to keep the keys to the grim safety deposit box, plus a letter (witnessed by a lawyer) authorizing the bank to release the contents of the safety deposit box, over the bank's dead body.

You may of course choose to wear the safety deposit box keys on a matching chain around your neck, but as costume jewelry it is not everyone's first choice.

Thinking Young

"You're only as old as you feel." A dubious criterion, this, especially if you feel about a hundred and twenty.

Also, to be one of the young at heart, you need to associate mostly with juveniles. Not easy to do. If you hang around playgrounds, you draw suspicion as a child molester. You have to limit the potential for getting arrested by trying to get noticed by young *adults*. Marathon runs, for example, provide a milieu that attracts thousands of people young enough to make an older participant forget his years for at least the first fifty yards, with the option of dropping dead in a good cause.

Another tip: try not to become agitated about being the only member of your family who is not smoking pot. On a regular basis. The physical side effects of moral indignation — tightly pursed lips, permanently raised eyebrows, etc. — merely isolate you from younger members of the community, as a *mouldy fig*. A *tsker*. True, *someone* has to speak up for the traditional values, but make sure it is someone else.

Don't be a martyr to the decline of Western civilization. Instead of audibly deploring young people's taste in popular music — i.e., rock, bop, rap, hip-hop, etc. — as a case of amps in their pants, try to see this dominance by primitive rhythms as a return to basics.

Always keep in mind that the main reason the younger generation has no respect for us is that our generation is personally responsible for global warming and the premature extinction of life on planet Earth.

When today's kid looks at a senior he sees the person to blame for the impending doom of the snowy owl.

Thanks to millions of younger school teachers, kids know that degradation of the world's environment is traced directly to anyone born before David Suzuki. We all wear the scarlet letter of Hawthorne's heroine, scorned by this new breed of Puritans who see us damned for eating meat, living in houses made of slaughtered forest, frequenting that den of ecological iniquity, the gas station.

For the young, the vehicle of divine justice is the skateboard. Which can pursue the perfidious old person even unto the sidewalk and beyond.

This is why the senior should minimize any outward sign of maturity. That can mean restricting our social life to exchanging e-mail with someone living in a largely unpopulated area of Siberia. Yet, sooner or later, what we see in the mirror is going to be seen by someone else. Who hurriedly crosses himself, or otherwise indicates that our appearance is classified as for mature adults only.

Face it, Dad: the highway to Heaven is closed to anyone pushing sixty-five.

Death Can Be Fatal

The most common killer among the elderly — according to the obituary notices at least — is *natural causes*. Natural causes are what most of us are going to die of. Yet natural causes are never listed in the medical texts that constitute the library of the average paranoid senior.

This makes it a lot harder to avoid incurring one, or more, of these "natural causes." Unnatural causes of death, yes, we understand that being run over by an SUV is not a natural phenomenon, except in parts of Italy, even though the manufacturers of that vehicle may have us believe that it is a merciful, even prestigious, quietus for the elderly.

Other unnatural causes of demise among the elderly include:

- unprovoked attack by a Murphy bed,
- removing the hearing aid before walking along railway tracks, and
- using the electric razor in the shower.

However, there is no warning label on a natural cause of death. This means that the oldster has little chance of avoiding something that hasn't really been identified, as compared to the hazard of standing under a falling piano. When the senior wakes up in the morning (already a freaky occurrence) his first thought is not "Hey, today I'd better watch out for a natural cause of death!"

Nor may he reasonably expect his family doctor to inform him that he has contracted a natural cause of death. The physician is trained to tap dance around that kind of diagnosis, implying as it does that modern medical science has failed to cope with the most common of fatal conditions.

This of course makes it that much harder to be immortal, without giving up chocolate.

In this respect it would be comforting to be able to believe that there is a real Dr. Frankenstein out there somewhere, beavering away at cheating those darned natural causes with a charge of man-made lightning.

However, the reality is that, though every human life is precious, on paper at least, after sixty-five that life loses about 10 percent in value per year. After ninety, all the collateral is spent and a person is living on borrowed time — one kind of lending that draws no interest.

So Who Needs Us?

Everybody wants to feel needed. No one, regardless of age, likes to wake up in the morning with the thought: "Shit, I'm as useless as tits on a bull."

Even if a person is wanted only by the police, it's something. But old folks are rarely found on a wanted list, being too fragile to commit any offence except watering the lawn on a proscribed day.

The irony is that the more needed a person felt, when young, the greater the shock of now being redundant. This is a strong argument for having lived a life that avoided service to anyone but oneself. In politics, for instance. Old politicians have no problem with exchanging public life for the self-serving. But the loss of feeling needed can hit old ladies who haven't avoided motherhood — which was easier for guys. Hence their altruistic physical activities like running a thirty-mile marathon in aid of finding a cure for dandruff.

For some seniors it is too late to learn how to be actively selfish. Old registered nurses, for instance, have often developed a dependency on ministering to other people. They retire badly, often hanging around the SPCA kennels, trying hard to get their caregiving fix by walking a three-legged dog, adopting a blind owl, etc.

Other oldsters satisfy the need urge by hugging a tree. As our primeval forests are still being threatened by logging, they provide a venue for protesters, including a large percentage of seniors. Old ladies, in particular, find it more rewarding to be carried off by a couple of policemen than to have no sex life at all. And the elderly man who has lost his wife finds solace in being chained to a tree. (Note: very rarely does a judge dare to sentence an elderly protester to more than a month of house arrest. Which is the accused's normal environment anyhow.)

Another venue heavily dependent on seniors who have nothing better to do is the civic/provincial/federal political government forum. This may seem to be a tedious way of getting seen — albeit briefly in a TV panning shot — but it is essential to projecting the image of democratic process. Very often these photo ops include the organizers' bribe of free coffee and cookies, so that the politically active senior gets to save on his food bill.

Finally, seniors play a role in the nation's economy, spending more than we earn and providing income for millions of tradesmen, healthcare workers, pharmacists, etc. If everyone were under sixty-five, the country would be bankrupt in no time.

Also, registered retirement plans depend on our hopping the twig at age ninety. Die young and we bugger up our portfolio.

Thus there is no reason for a senior to feel glum about being a burden on society. Society is carrying the much heavier load of Generation Y. As in yahoo.

Welcome to the Second (or More) Childhood!

According to demographics as projected by experts in the field, by the year 2500 *everybody* will be over sixty-five. This could mean that the experts should get out of the field and into town more often.

Or, they could be right. Thanks to faster automobiles and daytime television, all the younger generation may be either eliminated or prematurely aged, depending on whether they also got married.

But first we must stop calling people "old" just because they have a lot of years on the meter. "Elderly" is less offensive, "mature" better still, "seasoned" almost complimentary. And just because a seasoned person's ambulation leans towards totter-ing is no reason to think of him or her as "old." That person may just be drunk. (Alcohol is a pre-servative whose effects on locomotion are often misread as decrepitude.)

In the past it has been considered polite to refer to a woman who has survived youth as "a lady of a certain age." Today that phrase qualifies as libel. It violates the boomer credo: old age is something that will happen over my dead body.

Seniors also have the satisfaction of statistics that show them to have more political clout than any other group. Long after they have started hav-ing trouble remembering their own name, they can still put an X on an election ballot. Political parties have to be "elder-friendly" if they want to have a hope of gaining power. (It is significant that Canada's latest prime minister, Paul Martin, has started his career as top banana at age sixty-five. There is also talk of raising the age of retirement for members of the Senate from seventy-five to ninety, possibly even one hundred — a glimpse of Eternity, from Parliament Hill.

This proves that a person is never too old to become a politician, as long as he avoids attracting the attention of a coroner.

Also documented is that older persons' brains have lost little of their ability to understand a joke. A test group of seniors was exposed to the bogus hotel sign: "Guests are invited to take advantage of the chambermaid." Nearly all the seniors recognized this as humour. The rest wanted to know whether the hotel had an elevator.

Thus the evidence indicates that most older folk depend on their sense of humour as first line of defense against suicide. They prefer to expedite their demise by more congenial means, such as:

- eating too much fatty food,
- eating too little fatty food, or
- eating *anything* described as "food to die for."

Yes, it may be harder for the boomer generation to adjust, to greet old age cordially, after all those years of gambolling in green pastures. But you owe it to generations X, Y, and (shortly) Z to demonstrate that longevity is not necessarily a mistake, if not overdone.

Remember: nothing should be carried to excess, including moderation.

R_X: *Divine Intervention*

The key to growing old gracefully is to make sure that you have a good relationship with God. Which should be initiated *before* the ambulance arrives. The death-bed conversion has a success rate somewhere down there with that of Japan's national basketball team.

This rule is implied by the Holy Bible's account of the longevity of Methuselah, who lived to be 969. Now, if you are bothered by arthritis, or work as an insurance broker, the prospect of living for almost a millennium could strike you as depressing.

But check out Genesis 5:27: "And Methuselah lived an hundred eighty and seven years, and begat Lamech. And Methuselah lived after he begat Lamech seven hundred eighty and two years, and begat sons and daughters."

Now to be still begetting hundreds of years after reaching 187 speaks well for Meth's vital signs. But he lucked out in having the Almighty as his personal trainer. Thus he was still swinging when Lamech fathered Noah, whose sponsorship by God saved humanity and other critters from the worst precipitation recorded outside the Vancouver area.

Today, men commonly don't enlist God till we've wasted a lot of money on Chinese herbal remedies that promise longevity. We think we are getting results because our skin turns yellow. But there is no clinical evidence that chewing ginseng roots will enable us to stick around long enough to catch the next ark.

Also suggested is that, if you hope to match Meth by turning to God, it's best to start before your neck is too stiff to make the move. It is well known that there are no atheists in the foxholes or the Emergency waiting room. Only the young and healthy can afford to discount the existence of a Supreme Being other than Wayne Gretzky.

As we age, agnosticism gradually lowers its raised eyebrow. Hades, as a forwarding address, seems less apocryphal. Heaven, an affordable destination. (Most old folk don't give much thought to Purgatory as other than a kind of drive-through soul-wash.)

Very few of us expect to be shunted into the lane that is access to Hell — paved with good intentions and downhill all the way. Reason: we believe that sin is *genetic*. Even mortal sin is curable, if caught early enough (before ninety).

Also it is possible to get saved in the comfort of our own home, thanks to TV evangelists who wedge salvation between the Sunday football and reruns of *I Love Lucy*.

So, there is no reason for an old person to fear damnation, just because it is urged by other motorists. If by your works ye shall be judged, the thing to do is to make a list of your good works, over a lifetime, and rate yourself out of ten for each of the following:

1. *Cleanliness.* (Next to godliness.)
2. *Punctuality.* (Early for everything but your wedding.)
3. *Temperance.* (Never drunk in a public place before lunch.)

A total score of fifteen or better should assure the oldster of getting a fair hearing before St. Peter. But to be on the safe side, guys, better get rid of that old, grainy video of Tessie the Tassel Twirler.

The Plus Side of Dotage

The physical benefits of exceeding sixty-five include a natural immunity to certain conditions: acne, nocturnal emissions, diaper rash (usually). Also, the old person enjoys *acquired immunity* to: measles, temptation (other than chocolate), long-term mortgage, street racing....

The most obvious plus for the three-score-and-tenner: some younger people respect *grey hair*. As long as it isn't theirs, of course. A younger person will hold open a door for grey hair, more or less obliging you to enter some place whether you planned to or not.

You are not expected to rescue a maiden in distress. Any residual impulse to do so is suppressed by doubt that the distressed party is a maiden, if aged ten years or older. (Note: For an old guy, his trying to catch any woman who appears to be fainting requires further study, as she is apt to topple him with her to the ground, creating a scene that is subject to misinterpretation, possibly police arrest.)

But the most valuable advantage of all is that the older person has gained *experience*. Whether he or she has *learned* from experience is a matter of intelligence plus absence of temptation — easier for a smart Tibetan monk.

In any event, life has taught the codger certain lessons that are part of the post-graduate course of survival. Some of these lessons are gender-specific.

For example, the elderly lady has learned:

- beauty is only skin deep, but guys don't dig the sub-dermal;
- a bar is not the best place to meet a gentleman who shares your interest in metaphysics;
- wearing spike heels to bed can compromise more than your feet;
- chivalry, though not dead, is on life support; and
- the knight in shining armour has rusted out.

Similarly, the old gent has learned:

- a bar is not the best place to meet a girl with an IQ higher than that of a gerbil;
- not taking "No!" for an answer is the first sign of mental decline;
- Calvin Klein is not the Saviour;
- personal integrity cannot survive the use of hair dye; and
- yellow undershorts don't need to be laundered as often.

But the best part of being old — for both genders — is that we are no longer middle-aged. Middle age is a nondescript period of life. We would save ourselves a lot of blahs if we could jump straight from youth to seniorhood, without those draggy years (forty to sixty-four) when we are fixated on saving enough money to afford to be a living fossil.

It is now too late to worry about that. We are either financially comfortable or living in an abandoned piano crate. We can concentrate on life's little pleasures, which don't come any smaller.

Finally, the old person enjoys the distinction of being a survivor. No mean feat, this, when we consider how many times we have piloted a supermarket cart down an aisle bristling with organically grown veggies. Or eaten at a bus depot. If we think of life as the *Titanic*, we seniors are the ones who clawed our way into a lifeboat. It might have been nice to finish the journey in a private yacht, but remember: it is easier for a camel to pass through the eye of a needle, than for a person to get into a really surefire investment portfolio.

What *is* certain is that by exceeding the age limit we have helped to prove how much human longevity has increased in the last thousand years, with the help of duct tape.

We are still being outlived by the Galapagos tortoise, but the turtle has been able to lay eggs and walk away from them, whereas we've had *family*.

So, boomer, it's show time. Break a leg!